How My Ordinary Became Extraordinary

Teri Benson

DEDICATION

To Dallin, Jace, and McCall

CONTENTS

ACKNOWLEDGMENTS

On an ordinary day in October 2012, a small, seemingly insignificant chest pain changed my life forever. This book is the true story of my grueling recovery from an aortic dissection in my heart.

I am forever grateful for an amazing surgeon, Dr. Schorlemmer, and his team, who worked for over eighteen hours to save my life.

I thank my Father in Heaven for the healing power of prayer and for all of the miracles that took place to let me keep living. I can't express how grateful I am for a rare second chance at life.

I want to express my love and gratitude to my amazing family and friends for being there for me during this very challenging recovery.

Thank you to Mike for believing in me and for making my dream for this book come true. And to Amy, thank you for all your patience and your amazing talent for helping me tell my story.

To Dallin, Jace, and McCall, you are so strong and truly amazing. I am so proud of you. I am so blessed to still be here and to be your mom. I love you guys sooooo much!

PROLOGUE

Sunday Morning, October 28

When I woke from the dead, the first thing I heard was a beeping sound. At first I thought it might be an alarm clock, but then hums, whirs, and other noises joined in—sounds that didn't belong in my bedroom. This wasn't right. Where was I?

I opened my eyes to see a sterile-looking room, filled with strange equipment and computers, all of them making noise. I blinked as my brain tried to catch up with what was happening. Was I in a computer lab? How did I get here?

I realized I was lying in a bed, with miles of cords and IVs connecting me to the machinery like something out of a science fiction movie. I could feel something sticking out of my neck with a grip like a claw, but I didn't know what it was. A handful of tubes ran down my torso into my stomach, disappearing under the blankets. Another tube stuck out of my nose. I felt detached from my body, but I knew something was terribly wrong. Nobody else was in the room. For whatever reason, I'd been left here. I couldn't remember why.

I needed to go home. I needed to find answers.

But first I just needed to climb out of the bed. *Okay, Teri,* I told myself, *you just need to grab the handrail on the bed and pull yourself up.*

I lifted my arm to reach for the rail.

Pain exploded across my arm as if someone had just smashed it with a sledgehammer. My arms shook, and I felt weaker than I'd ever felt in my life. I looked at my hands and saw that they were swollen so big that I could barely move my fingers. My mind raced. My heart pounded. What had happened to me?

I couldn't stay here. I had to escape. I had to get away from this, whatever it was. I eyed the bed railing and decided on option two. If I

1

rolled over and lifted my leg over the rail, then I could use it to push myself up. I brought my other arm across my body to grab the rail to help me roll onto my side. Pain washed over that arm, too, but I gritted my teeth. I could do this. I could do this…

The PAIN…UGH, the pain! Every part of me screamed for relief.

Closing my eyes, I made one last desperate grab for the rail. My puffy fingers closed around the metal bar. YES! Now I just needed to lift my leg up and over. My skin felt clammy and my entire body trembled with the effort. Almost there. Almost there.

"Where are you trying to go?" cried a female voice. I looked up and saw a woman in scrubs rushing over to me. Her brown hair was pulled back and her badge said her name was Brooke. I recognized that she must be a nurse. That meant I was in a hospital. Why?

Tears welled up in my eyes as I lay there clutching the rail. "I just need to go home," I whispered. It hurt to get the words out. My mouth and throat felt dry and tender, like I hadn't used them in days. How long had I been here?

"You're not going anywhere," said Brooke as she lifted me back to a reclined position and adjusted the cords and tubes around the bed. "You need to be here. You've been through a lot of trauma. You're very sick. We're here to help you, but you need to stay calm."

I felt so tired that I gave up and let her move me. My thoughts tried to break through the fuzzy feeling in my head and figure out what happened. A few flashes of memory came to mind—pain, a car ride to the hospital, a man in scrubs speaking to me, my daughter's tear-filled face, more pain—but I couldn't put the pieces together. The tears kept flowing as I started to drift off. *Please just let me go home*, I thought. *Please just let this be a dream.*

My eyes closed. The beeps and hums of the medical machines faded. A floating sensation slowly filled my whole body, and the pain evaporated, melting away into the air. Ohhh, yes. I remembered where I was before this—a place so beautiful that words couldn't describe it. It was more like a feeling than an image, an overwhelming sense of joy and well-being. It felt like someone had turned love into a blanket and wrapped me up in it. I had been there, and I never wanted to leave.

I could see it all around me again now. I reached out to grasp it, but it slipped through my fingers.

I wanted to go back there. I wanted to stay there forever, in that world of light and endless sunrises.

Instead, I fell asleep. I woke later to a world of nightmares.

1
JUST A LITTLE CHEST PAIN

Five days earlier
Tuesday, October 23

Beeping filled the room, pulling me out of sleep. "Noooo…" I groaned, slapping at the alarm clock. The red lights displayed six thirty, the start of another day, but I felt like I'd only had an hour or two of rest. I finally slammed my hand down on the snooze button and silenced the horrible noise.

Ten minutes later, I hit the button again.

Another ten minutes, another snooze.

After half an hour went by, I decided I really should get up. The thought of going to work made me groan and bury my head under the blanket. So much paperwork. So much mediocrity. So much ordinariness.

"I need to make a change," I said to myself. "Find a new job or something." I needed something to revitalize my life. I needed to do something new, something challenging and unexpected.

I glanced at the clock and groaned again. First I just needed to get out of bed and take care of my responsibilities. Revolutionizing life would have to wait until later. Maybe next week.

After I forced myself through my morning routine and made it to the office, the day crawled by like any other. I sat at my desk, doing whatever I could to keep busy, and watched the clock. I closed out a few files that had been paid in full and prepared bills of sale to send to clients. I talked with coworkers. I ate lunch. I did more work. I made it through.

When five o'clock finally arrived, I decided to stop at the gym on my way home and run on the treadmill. I considered skipping the exercise for one day, but the routine was good for me, and I knew I'd feel better if I followed through. Discipline, Teri, discipline.

I decided to run four miles of sprint intervals rather than my full workout. As I fell into the rhythm of my running, allowing my thoughts to focus only on my movement, I felt some of the stress of the day melt away. Those few minutes of quiet solitude, just me and the treadmill, always gave me an energy boost and helped calm my mind.

It was hard to believe that one year ago I was just starting this regimen, and now I was in the best shape of my life—such a big change over such a short period of time. It was a difficult period of time, definitely. Maintaining a workout schedule is never easy. But seeing the results made it more than worthwhile. I may have felt stagnant in other areas of life, but at least I had my health.

That evening as I was getting ready for bed, a small, stinging pain erupted right in the middle of my chest, about the size of a fifty-cent piece. I reached to touch it, wondering what it could be. Some kind of heartburn? What did I eat earlier? Nothing spicy—maybe it was just indigestion? It was uncomfortable, but I decided it would probably pass. I needed to sleep if I wanted to be awake at work the next day.

After lying in bed for several minutes with the pain not subsiding, I started to feel a little irritated. It was late, I was exhausted, and I could see the clock numbers ticking away the time I had left before I needed to be up again. Yet the pain wouldn't go away, and my worries grew.

Frustrated, I grabbed my iPad and searched for "stinging pain in chest." Nothing specific came up, but I found plenty of recommendations to "see your doctor for any kind of chest problem." By this point, it was one thirty in the morning, so seeing my regular doctor was out. I thought about other possibilities, but decided I was making a big deal out of nothing. This was ridiculous, I thought. I lay back down and shut my eyes, determined not to let the pain keep me from resting.

"Get up."

My eyes opened. What was that?

"Get up, go put on your sweats, and have McCall take you to the ER."

My heart started racing. I knew that voice. It was the voice of my dad, who had passed away ten years earlier. I didn't know if I was actually hearing him speak or if it was just in my mind, but the stern tone told me I needed to obey.

I went to find McCall, my nineteen-year-old daughter and youngest child. She was still awake (teenagers…) and I asked her to drive me to the ER. She wasted no time in getting up and getting dressed while I waited for her downstairs.

While I was waiting, my middle child, Jace, came to see what was going on. "What's up, Mom?" he asked, blinking sleep out of his blue eyes.

I blushed. It all felt silly when I had to say it out loud. "I have this stupid little stinging pain in my chest, and I just want to get it checked. I'm having McCall run me over to the ER."

His forehead creased with worry. "Should I come with you guys?"

"No, it's no big deal," I said. "We'll be back in an hour or two. Just go back to bed."

He nodded and returned to his room just as McCall came bounding down the stairs, her long blonde hair tied back and a sweatshirt hiding her slight frame. "All set," she said. "Let's go."

The drive to the ER only took about ten minutes. The waiting room was empty as we walked in. Apparently it was a slow night for emergencies.

"How can I help you?" asked the nurse at the desk.

I told her I had a small pain in my chest, and while it was probably nothing, I just wanted to be sure. "I know it's not a heart attack," I said. "I had one of those three and a half years ago, and this feels nothing like it."

She nodded. "Follow me, please."

She took us into a room and checked my blood pressure, which was normal. Then she had me change into a hospital gown. I reluctantly stripped down, wondering if maybe I shouldn't have bothered coming in. This was an awful lot of fuss for a minor chest pain. I refused to put on the hospital non-skid socks. They looked silly. McCall tied up the back of the gown, and I seated myself on the bed. McCall began folding up my clothes and sticking them in the bag left by the nurse.

I laughed. "McCall, you don't need to put my clothes away. We're not going to be here that long."

She shrugged. "I already put them in there. You can get them out again later."

A moment later the doctor came in and listened to my heartbeat. "Do you have a heart murmur?" he asked with an unreadable expression.

"No."

He kept moving the stethoscope around my chest and back, still giving no indication of his thoughts. "I want you to have your blood work done," he finally said.

"Uh...okay."

A nurse came in and drew four vials from my arm, then left with the doctor. McCall and I sat and waited. The stinging grew worse. We waited some more. McCall started to become frustrated, and I could tell she was tired. So was I. Maybe this was a mistake. I just wanted to go back to bed.

He finally came back in. "Your blood work looks fine. No enzymes peaking, blood markers look good."

Yay! That meant I could leave.

He paused. "I want to get a quick CT scan, though, just to make sure."

The nurse came back with a wheelchair to take me for the scan. She looked at my attire and said, "I need you to put on the socks."

I gave in, now thinking about something that I found even more unnecessary. "I really don't need a wheelchair. I can walk. Especially with these safety socks."

McCall rolled her eyes. "Mom, just get in the wheelchair so we can go home."

I sighed and complied, feeling ridiculous as the nurse wheeled me to the CT room. Really, this was all so much overkill.

However, laying there and listening to the machine whirr and hum as it analyzed me, I started to feel the first flickers of fear. What if they found a problem? What would that mean? I blinked to clear my eyes. I would not cry.

This was ridiculous. Nothing was wrong. And if there was, it couldn't be anything that bad. Maybe just a minor complication from my previous heart attack. Nothing I couldn't handle.

I waited in the room with McCall while the doctor looked over the results. When he came back in, his face had a serious expression. He explained some medical jargon that I didn't quite understand, but his last sentence caught my attention fully. "An ambulance is on its way here," he said. "It's going to transport you to St. Mark's Hospital. You need to have open heart surgery tonight."

Wait.

What?

Open heart surgery?

Did he just say *open heart* surgery?

WHAT?

They're going to cut my chest open? Why?

What does this mean?

No, this can't be right.

You're really going to cut my chest open?

No. *No.* Why could I possibly need this?

As panicked thoughts raced through my head, I tried to force myself to stay calm. I looked at McCall and swallowed. "Well...this can't be good." Neither of us laughed, and the tension in the room thickened.

They started an IV in both of my arms and put some sort of oxygen thing on my finger. There was a red light on it, and I tried to concentrate on that instead of the fear I was feeling. It reminded me of science fiction movies, so I made another attempt to lighten the mood. I raised my finger and showed it to McCall. "ET phone home."

She laughed, and it broke some of the anxiety we were both feeling. "Do that again. I need to video it." So I did, and we both laughed together. I felt a little calmer. I would be fine. Everything was going to be all right.

After that, my memory went blank.

***

A glimpse of my nephew Ethan leaning up against the wall.

What was he doing here?

Blank spots.

People in scrubs, their heads covered with hats and masks, looking down at me. One of them was my friend's daughter-in-law. I made the bridal jewelry for her wedding. I recognized her beautiful brown eyes.

"I know you."

More blank spots.

A place of unimaginable beauty.

Familiar faces...but who were they?

Where was I?

Why couldn't I touch the ground?

So warm and peaceful. Love surrounding me.

Amazing, brilliant colors.

Indescribable beauty rushing by me.

The most exquisite flowers I'd ever seen.

I had never felt like this before.

I knew I was in the presence of something very powerful.

"Can I stay here forever?"

I reached for them, stretching as far as possible.

Something pulled me back.

Pain.

Unbelievable pain.

Darkness

2
AFTERMATH

Sunday, October 28

The next thing I saw was McCall's face. When she noticed my eyes open, she lit up with joy. "Mom? Mom! You're okay!"

"What's happening?"

"You've had heart surgery, Mom."

WHAT?

Where was I?

Why couldn't I move?

What happened?

I took a look around. Tubes, monitors, and IVs filled the room and the bed. My two sons, Dallin and Jace, stood near McCall and my mom. My brothers, Wayne and David, were near the door. Everyone looked both terrified and relieved.

Why were they here? Why was *I* here? Everything seemed like a messy blur.

One feeling broke through all the chaos—my throat burned with a desperate thirst. The roof of my mouth felt like sand. Before anything else could be sorted out, I knew I needed something to drink. "I'm thirsty," I said, expecting one of my kids to help me.

No one moved, so I couldn't tell if I'd gotten the words out. "Hello? I need water."

McCall spoke softly. "You can't have any water yet."

What? Why not? I was dying of thirst! My thoughts jumbled together. How did I get here? Why wouldn't they let me drink anything? Were they trying to kill me? I needed to get out of there. I had no idea what was going on, but I knew I needed some water or I was going to die.

"Please get me water. Please, please get me water."

David stepped closer to the bed. "We want to give you a blessing."

The movement scared me, and I tried to shrink away. "Don't touch me! You're trying to kill me." I licked my dry, cracked lips. "Get me some water or just let me die."

"Teri, we just want to give you a blessing," said David.

"No. You can give me a blessing if you get me water."

"The nurse said you can't have water yet."

"I don't care. I need it."

He kept talking, but I didn't listen. Instead, I fought with my unrelenting thirst and tried to remember what had happened and why my family was now torturing me. The last thing I remembered was taking McCall to the ER. But if that was true, why was I the one hooked up to all of the machines?

I tried to move again, and pain set my entire chest on fire. I groaned under the onslaught. What was causing that? What had happened to me? What was going on? My vision started swimming with dark spots. I couldn't keep my eyes open, and I finally succumbed to blackness.

***

When I woke up again, the room was quiet except for the noise of the machines and the computers. McCall was the only one there. She rushed over to the bed. "Mom, you're awake! How are you feeling?"

"What's going on? Can I have water yet?"

"Not yet. Mom, you can't get upset. We're not trying to kill you. Do you remember?"

I shook my head.

"I took you to the ER because you were having a strange pain in your chest. They said you needed surgery."

"Surgery? Why don't I remember that?"

"I don't know. Try to think back." She took out her phone and pulled up a video, then held it out so I could watch it play. "Do you remember this?"

It was a recording of me lying in a hospital bed. A contraption on my finger had a red light on the end of it. I held up my hand and mimicked a movie quote: "ET phone home." Then McCall and I both laughed, and then the short clip was over.

That little moment brought it all flooding back. "I remember that!" I exclaimed. "I *do* remember. I remember the pain." I looked down at my chest and saw a huge, sewn-up gash disappearing under the hospital gown, covered in medical tape. I looked like someone attached a zipper to the front of my body, and the sight made goose bumps rise across my skin. I

9

quickly averted my eyes.

"Mom." McCall's face looked serious. "You had something called an aortic dissection. The CT scan showed that your aorta had torn in several places and was tearing out of your aortic valve. You've been through two surgeries since you got here. You're so lucky to be alive!"

"Wait, two surgeries? How long have I been here?"

"Almost five days now. It's Sunday."

"What? Yesterday was Tuesday."

"No, mom. That was when we went to the ER. When they saw the images on the scan..." McCall's voice broke, but she kept going. "They rushed you here by ambulance, to St. Mark's Hospital. Do you remember Dr. Schorlemmer coming in to talk to you when we arrived?"

"No. Who's that?"

"Your surgeon. He explained what was happening. Jace and Dallin didn't make it in time to see you before you went in, but I..." McCall's eyes watered and tears began flowing down her cheeks. "Mom, you started telling me how much you loved me and how proud you were of me. I told you to stop and made you promise to pull through the surgery. And you said you would. You kept telling me over and over how much you loved me. You were crying, and so upset. And then they wheeled you away toward the operating room."

Realizing what my daughter had been through over the past few days made me sick to my stomach. I wanted to take her hand and brush the tears out of her eyes and comfort her, but I was still so weak that I could barely lift my arm.

"I was so scared," she continued. "I just couldn't lose you. That was the longest day of our lives."

"Our lives?" Was she talking about herself and her brothers? Who else had been here?

"There were a lot of us in the waiting room. The boys made it over, Grandma was here, Lora Lee, Julie, Paige, Wendi, Aunt Janice, Laura, Leslie, Lindsi, Rebecca, Uncle Wayne, Aunt Melissa, Uncle David, Aunt Amanda. People just kept coming in to support you. The nurses and doctors came out and gave us updates every so often, but it was never good news. Complications kept happening. The right side of your heart failed a couple different times. They..." She swallowed. "They weren't giving us much hope."

"After about ten hours, Dr. Schorlemmer took us to a private room and said they'd finished the surgery, but they still needed to do more work and that the next six to twelve hours were critical. They said if you didn't wake up during that time, t-that you never would.

"We were able to see you a few times since then. The second time, the nurse yelled, 'Teri, your kids are here to see you!' And you opened your eyes. It was just for a second, but I think that was when I knew you'd be okay. They only let one of us in at a time after that, but we've all spent time sitting with you. You had to go in for another surgery on Friday because your kidneys, colon, and liver were failing and they had to fix the arteries, but they said you made it through that one like a champ."

"How is it possible I went through all of that and don't remember anything?"

"I don't know, Mom. But I'm glad you're still here."

A nurse brought in some ice chips, and all thoughts of what McCall had been saying flew out of my head at the prospect of quenching my dying thirst. She told McCall I could only have six pieces. At that point, I'd take what I could get.

McCall fed me the first chip, and ohhhh, nothing had ever tasted so good. "More!" I insisted.

"Just take it slow, Mom. Try and stay calm."

She fed me the rest of the ice, but it wasn't anywhere near enough. "I need more."

McCall looked toward the nurse. "Can she?"

The nurse nodded. "Just a few more." She smiled at me. "I know your throat is dry, but I promise you're not going to die of thirst. You're being completely hydrated through your IVs." She injected something into one of the tubes. "This will help you calm down and get some sleep."

As I lay there, I thought about all the things McCall had told me. How I'd been here for five days. How I'd had multiple surgeries with slim chances. How they'd apparently nearly lost me. And all I could do was wonder how.

How could something like this happen? I was in the best shape of my entire life. I had worked and sweated and persevered for months—running, cycling, weight training, you name it. I'd obsessed over getting fit, and I'd finally achieved my goals. I knew what I was doing. I was heading in the right direction, at least physically. In some ways, that was all I had.

And now I was lying here, helpless and weakened. I hadn't been sick. I hadn't been in a car accident. It just sort of happened. How was that possible? For crying out loud, I ran four miles of sprints earlier the same day. I rode almost one hundred miles on my bike two weeks ago. How could this happen? How could this happen to *me*?

3
LEARNING TO BREATHE

Monday, October 29

I woke up to my nurse adjusting the machines around me. "Good morning," she said. "I have some good news for you. You can drink water and some clear juice today."

After feeling thirsty for so long, I thought it was the best news in the world. "Yay!"

She grinned at my excitement. "The doctor will be in shortly to see you." Before she left, she brought me a big hospital mug full of ice water and a disposable cup full of apple juice. She put in a straw in the juice and held it up to mouth.

I drank and drank and drank. It tasted amazing, and the moisture soothing my dry throat was pure heaven. Finally I wasn't distracted by my horrendous thirst. For some reason the juice made my belly full, but I didn't mind. Drinking liquids again was more than worth feeling a little stuffed.

A gray-haired man walked in, and I didn't recognize him. "Are you my doctor?" I asked.

"No, I'm Dr. Thorne. Dr. Schorlemmer is off today, but he'll be here to see you tomorrow. How are you feeling?"

"Eh..."

We discussed my current condition, and he commented, "You're looking much better. You are one tough little lady." He checked my vitals. "Your kidney, colon, and liver functions are looking amazingly good today. You'll be able to have some chicken broth and Jell-O."

As excited as I'd been about the water, I thought it was strange that drinking chicken broth was a milestone. It was just chicken broth.

I thanked him as he left, and my nurse, Brooke, came back in. "Dr.

Schorlemmer wants you to sit up and to try standing for a minute or two today."

"Okay," I said. How hard could that be?

"Oh, and we need to weigh you while you're up."

That sounded fine, too. After all, I was in the best shape of my life.

Another nurse came in with a portable scale and handrails. Both she and Brooke began moving the cords, tubes, IVs, oxygen, and other medical equipment out of the way so that I could move. I again noticed the tubes running down my front and into my stomach. What were those for? I considered asking if I could see where they were going, but changed my mind. I'd heard enough about what happened. I didn't want to know what the tubes were doing.

They removed two boot-like things from my legs, which I found out later were intended to help with my circulation. I caught my first glimpse of my feet and legs. Ew! My skin was a sickly yellow color, and my feet were swollen to the point that my toes looked ready to explode. I tried to move them, but they wouldn't budge. On my right leg I saw what looked like incisions and bruises, starting at my ankle and running up the inside of my leg all the way to my knee. What the crap? I thought the problem was in my chest.

"Why is my leg all cut up?" I asked.

"During the second surgery, they took an artery out of your leg to repair the failed ones," Brooke explained.

Not quite remembering everything McCall had told me, I felt confused. What was she talking about? What failed arteries? No, on second thought, I didn't want to know about that, either.

The bed started to move, adjusting me to a more upright position, closer to the floor. Then it lowered my legs until I was sitting up. I felt a little lightheaded, and I tried to move my arms to prop myself up. I looked down at them, and...ugh. My hands and arms were just as swollen as my legs, and they were that funky yellow color, too. All those IVs sticking out of me made me look like a pincushion.

"We're going to prop you up," said Brooke. "Here we go." She and the other nurse boosted me up from under my arms, very gently, until I was sitting at the edge of the bed with my feet touching the floor. Pain lanced across my chest, and I had to grit my teeth against it. If this was what sitting up felt like, how was I going to manage standing?

After a few minutes for me to get used to sitting, the nurses helped me stand on the scale.

It wasn't as hard as I'd been imagining.

It was much, much harder.

My feet and legs throbbed under my weight. My head swam with dizziness, and I could feel the blood rushing out of it. Every part of my body cried out for relief.

"Almost there," said Brooke as they helped me grab the hand rails on the scale. "Are you doing okay?"

"Yeah."

No.

"Okay. Hold on for just a sec. We have to let go so that the scale can measure your weight."

I concentrated on taking deep breaths, fighting off the whiteness trying to creep into the corners of my eyes. If I fell now, I didn't think I'd survive hitting the floor.

It felt like forever, but it was only a second or two before Brooke announced, "Got it."

I looked down at the scale and blinked when I saw the red number. 178. I closed my eyes and opened them again, sure that I was seeing things because of how lightheaded I felt. Still 178.

"Is that how much I weigh?" I asked.

"Yes, it is," Brooke said. "You have some extra water weight from the surgeries. It's just temporary."

They helped me to sit back on the bed, but I felt so faint that I could barely think. How could I weigh 178 pounds? I was supposed to weigh 130. This couldn't be right. I was fat now? What had they done to me? All my hard work for the past year, gone in the blink of an eye.

I felt tears pool in my eyes again. Was this just a bad dream? A dream where I couldn't even stand up for more than a few seconds? A dream where I weighed more than I ever had before, even when I was nine months pregnant? Some dim part of me realized that my weight was the least of my current problems, but 178 was such a specific number. It was a quantifiable measure of just how much had changed over the last few days, and that scared me. I didn't want to think about it. I couldn't face the scope of what my body had endured.

I saw both Dallin and Jace over the course of the day, and they assured me that I was doing great and would be fine. Outwardly I agreed. I didn't want them to worry; they'd been through enough. Inwardly, I felt disturbed that my too-ordinary life had now become far too extra-ordinary.

***

Tuesday, October 30

Breakfast happened the next day. Brooke placed a tray in front of me with oatmeal, some fruit, yogurt, juice, and toast. I wasn't very hungry, plus it was painful to navigate my way through the tray with all of the IVs sticking out of me. Some yogurt and a little fruit, and I felt stuffed. At least I was eating real food, I reasoned.

A gray-haired man in scrubs entered the room, though not the same man as the previous day. He had sunglasses pushed up on his head and reading glasses hanging down on his nose. He smiled when he saw that I was awake. "Hi, Teri. Do you remember who I am?"

The heartfelt way he looked at me gave it away. Feeling the magnitude of what I'd been through—what he had brought me through—wash over me, I started to cry. I wanted to jump up and hug him, to somehow convey all of the gratitude I felt welling up inside me, but since I couldn't move, I settled for expressing myself with words. Through my tears I said, "No, but I know who you are. You are the man who saved my life."

He stepped closer to the bed and put his hand on the railing. I had the feeling that he understood everything I wanted to convey. "Well, Teri," he said, "you are my miracle."

My mind was too fuzzy to retain much of what we discussed. He said my progress was unbelievable, and that I was doing better than he had ever imagined. They would be able to remove some of the IVs and tubes, which would allow my body to start working on its own again. We talked a little more, and then he left so that I could rest. That short conversation made me feel more at peace than I had since waking up in the hospital.

Thinking about all of the equipment connecting to my body, I wondered what I looked like, sure that my appearance must be awful. I felt that my hair was pulled off my neck, and I reached up to see why that was. They couldn't have cut off my hair, could they?

Instead of the short hair I feared, I found a lovely French braid. Now who had done that?

One of my nurses, Jen, walked in, and I asked her who braided my hair.

"I did," she said. "I wanted you to look pretty for your family and friends."

Her kindness touched me. "Wow, thank you."

"I've got some good news," she said. "I'm going to remove the swan IV from your neck and the tubes from your stomach."

"Sweet." I couldn't wait to be rid of that awful claw-like thing next to my head.

She pulled up the edges of the adhesive patch holding the huge IV in my neck. She told me to take a deep breath. I did, and she pulled the patch off in one movement.

"Ow!" It felt like the skin came off with it, and that was only the adhesive. The other bits of tape attaching the claw thing didn't hurt so much, but I dreaded the removal of the actual device.

"We need to take a practice run," Jen told me. "Breathe in. Now breathe out. Good. One more time. Okay, breathe in, then breathe out, then breathe in again, and that's when I'll do it."

Holy. Crap. This was going to hurt. Gritting my teeth, I breathed in, let it out, and then inhaled again.

Jen moved. A sharp, stabbing pain surged through my neck. I squeezed my hands into fists and gasped.

"Breathe out," Jen said.

"I can't!" I hissed. "The pain…"

"Breathe out. It's over. Just relax."

When I finally managed to release the breath I was holding, I looked at what she'd pulled out. The part that had been in my neck stretched four inches long. I couldn't even fathom how it had fit inside me. My neck throbbed as she held pressure on the hole and bandaged it up.

"You're doing great," she said. "Now let's get the tubes out."

She pulled up my gown, exposing my stomach, and I lost my breath as I saw it. The three tubes going into my abdomen were not small, little tubes like I'd expected. They were large. Very, very large. I felt a sense of nausea. Did I have to be awake for this?

"Okay, same thing," said Jen. "Breathe in, breathe out, breathe in, and I'll get them out."

We took a practice run. I felt myself starting to sweat. Now for the real thing.

I breathed in, out, and in, feeling close to panic. She held my stomach firmly and pulled all three out at once, and my guts felt like they were yanked out along with the tubes. I wanted to scream, but I couldn't let the air out of my lungs.

"Breathe out," said Jen, keeping pressure on the opening. "Breathe out."

I finally managed it, and Jen began putting medical strips over the wounds. "You did an awesome job," she said. "These will heal up nicely."

I looked down to see the results and was confronted by what looked like three bullet holes. *Great*, I thought, *more scars*. In light of everything else, I knew I shouldn't worry about that, but the sight still made my skin crawl.

"You're making amazing progress," said Jen as she took one of the IVs out of my right hand. "We're so happy."

Looking at my hand, so bruised, swollen, and ugly, I couldn't understand her excitement. Was this how I was going to look now? Was this now my life? Were my accomplishments going to consist of drinking chicken broth, standing up, and not passing out when they pulled another needle out of my body?

Exhausted from the ordeal, I drifted in and out throughout the day. My kids, friends, and family members passed through, but it all became a blur. Everyone told me how amazing and beautiful I was. Lunch came. Dinner came. I didn't feel like eating, but the juice and water were nice. My throat felt dry all the time, like it had been burnt.

The things I remember are a bit surreal. At some point, someone commented, "Nice bathroom you've got here." I looked over and saw a toilet with a curtain you could pull around it. Yeah, nice bathroom.

It occurred to me that I'd been drinking quite a bit, so when a nurse next came in, I asked, "Shouldn't I need to get up and go to the bathroom?"

She laughed. "You have a catheter." Then she showed me the container where all my pee was going. Oh. Duh. I laughed, too.

A bit later, Jen returned with another nurse. "We're going to give you a sponge bath, and then I'll redo your French braid. It'll help you feel better. And you can brush your teeth."

I hadn't brushed my teeth the entire time? I had to have the worst breath in the world.

She washed my face and brought my bed to a sitting position so she could wash the rest of my body. It felt awkward to have someone else cleaning me, but the nurse made me feel at ease. I realized she'd been caring for me for a week now, so this wasn't the first time she'd seen me anyway. So instead of worrying about that, I tried to relax. The warm water felt amazing.

I glanced down at my body, afraid of what I would see. I didn't even recognize it. The scars, the bruises, the extra weight, the swelling…how could that be me? How could that be the body I had to live in? I looked away and focused on the wall instead. It was too much to handle. I couldn't accept it.

Jen asked, "Do you feel like you can stand?"

"Yes," I answered. The truth was, I didn't know, but I was not going to let that hideous body defeat me. I had to get back to normal, and standing was very normal.

"Okay, we're going to get you in a standing position for a minute so we can finish washing you."

They helped me to stand up, and I shook badly. Despite feeling weak, I managed to stay upright until the bath was done. Deep breaths in, deep breaths out.

After they gave me a fresh gown and changed my bed sheets, Jen brushed out my hair and braided it again. After days and days of lying in the same place in the same hospital gown, I felt wonderfully refreshed. She brought me a toothbrush, a cup of water, and a spit tray. The roof of my mouth burned and my tongue felt raw as I brushed, but it felt good anyway. My arm grew fatigued quickly, so I finished up, and the nurses helped me return to the bed.

I lay down as the hospital bed reclined again, my elation at being clean mixing with my irritation at how hard it was to do such simple things. It couldn't stay like this. There was no way. It was difficult now, but surely things would get better soon. Just like when I'd started working out, like all the other challenges I'd overcome in my life, I had to persevere.

I drifted off again, feeling that wonderful, pain-free sensation of floating. Breathe in, breathe out. Breathe in, breathe out. It would all be over soon.

4

FIRST STEPS

Wednesday, October 31

That night, I became aware of just how often my nurse was in my room. At least once an hour, someone came in to check on me, read my vital signs, and do other things that, while quick, still kept me from sleeping deeply. It was also very noisy. I could tell by the movement outside my door that I was right in front of the nurses' station. The bed felt uncomfortable, the oxygen tube in my nose was driving me crazy, and the pain made it hard to sleep. I just wanted to be in my own bed, where I could roll over on my side and curl up into a ball.

As I lay there awake, fear fluttered in my chest. How long had I been there? I didn't even know what day it was, and I couldn't quite remember everything that had happened to me. A horrible thought occurred to me—what about my job? Did they know I was in the hospital? I needed to call Laura and Ryan and tell them I wouldn't be in to work. But where was my phone? Did I leave it at the house? I just wanted to go home.

Despite the worries, I drifted off to sleep again.

Ahh. That beautiful place. I could see it. I drifted in the air as its breathtaking beauty flowed over me, just like before.

Wait. No, not over me. Past me. It didn't surround me anymore. I floated on the outside, looking in. I felt it barely touch me—a whisper of a caress as it flowed past and then continued farther and farther away. I wanted to call to it, ask it to come back, but there was nothing I could do.

Voices and the clatter of medical carts woke me. The sun streamed through my window, casting dancing shadows on the floor. A nurse's aide came in and wrote various notes on the whiteboard, then pulled another day off of the paper calendar.

October 31. It was Halloween already. I'd been there for over a week. How was that possible?

My nurse came in to check on me. "Good morning. You look great! How are you feeling?"

"I'm good," I answered. I would not admit how rattled this whole situation had left me.

"No one can believe the progress you're making," said the nurse. "Dr. Schorlemmer will be here in a while, and we'll find out what he wants you to do today. Your breakfast is here. Are you hungry?"

"A little bit." I instinctively tried to boost myself up with my hands, but she stopped me.

"You can't do that yet. Don't try to use your upper body." She propped me up with a pillow behind my back so that I could sit up.

Breakfast did not look appetizing, but the yogurt and fruit both looked good. My right arm still had the IV in it in case I needed it, but nothing was connected to it, so I could hold the yogurt and tear off the top without any help. My hands shook, but I did it. The smooth yogurt felt great on my raw mouth and throat. I ate some fruit, drank some water, and was full.

I noticed a TV up on the wall and looked around for a remote. The nurse pulled a pad out from beside my bed and told me that one button turned on the TV, while another would call the nurse's station if I needed someone.

I turned on the TV and flipped through the hospital info channels until I found the Today Show. Images of a breaking news story flitted past, and I watched, dumbfounded. Was that New York? Was that the Jersey Shore? What happened? The anchors announced that a hurricane had caused devastating damage, flooding, and deaths across the east coast. It looked horrible—so much destruction. Those poor people. After a few minutes, the tragedy began to overwhelm me, and I turned the TV off.

"How's my miracle girl?" Dr. Schorlemmer stood in the doorway, grinning at me.

I couldn't help but break into a big smile. "I'm good." This time, it wasn't so far from the truth. After all, I was alive, and for some reason seeing him made me feel more optimistic than I did on my own.

"You're making remarkable progress," he said. "Better than I could ever have imagined. It's almost unbelievable." He looked over my chart. "We can get you off a few more of these IVs, and the physical therapist will be in to see you later. I want you to get up and go for a little walk. We'll see how your oxygen levels stay today, and maybe we can get you off the nose tube tomorrow."

Great, great, great news all around. I began to hope that these first few days of recovery were the worst of it. I couldn't wait to get out of bed and go for a walk.

I dozed off for a while, until McCall came in to see me. I could tell from her face that they'd told her the good news. "Mom," she said, "you have so many people who want to come and see you. You've received a lot of flowers, but you can't have them in ICU, so we've taken them home. I took pictures of all of them to show you."

"Are you guys okay?" I asked. My boys were in their early twenties and McCall was nineteen, but I couldn't help wondering how they were managing at home.

"Yeah, we're good," McCall said. "Everyone is taking care of us. We have so much food in our house. You wouldn't believe how much love and support we have." She glanced at the calendar. "Can you believe it's Halloween today?"

I looked at my scarred and battered body. "At least it's a good day to look scary." We both laughed at that, and it felt good to make light of what had happened. I suddenly remembered my earlier question. "Oh, McCall, does my work know I'm here?"

She laughed. "Yes, they know. They're all pulling for you."

"Oh my gosh, and I'm supposed to host Bunco tomorrow night. Will you call someone, maybe Lauri, and tell her I probably won't be home to do it?"

"Don't worry. Everyone knows what happened."

I paused. "Everyone?"

"They've all been here supporting you. Don't worry about anything. We just want you to get better."

How did so many people know about this? More importantly, why did they know? Was it really that big a deal? I didn't want to be a burden to anyone, and I didn't want them to overreact. I was sure I'd be out of the hospital soon, and it seemed silly for everybody to get so worked up about it. "How does *everyone* know?"

McCall blushed. "Uh, well…Mom, please don't be mad. I know you hate putting stuff about yourself on Facebook, but I had to start posting about you there to let everyone know what was going on. All the phone calls were just too overwhelming. There were so many people who needed to know. Don't be upset."

At first I was livid. How embarrassing, to have this period of weakness broadcast to the whole world! Then I looked at my little girl, at the gauntness of her face. She was already thin, but the lack of sleep, the lack of food, and the overwhelming stress were taking a toll on her. It was such a huge responsibility for a nineteen-year-old. I couldn't imagine how she was coping.

She'd been through enough. I didn't need to cause her more pain. With tears in my eyes, I reassured her, "I'm not mad. You did the right thing."

She smiled with relief. "I put the ET phone home video on there. It was just so cute. I thought it would make everyone laugh."

"That's a good idea." I started to tear up and wiped my eyes before I could start crying. "Are the boys okay?"

"It's been hard for both of them, but they're doing better."

"I'm so sorry."

"Mom, we're just happy you're still here. Please don't worry. You need to stay calm."

I feel so blessed to have such amazing children—so lucky to be their mom. It reaffirmed my determination to get better quickly so that they didn't have to worry.

A little while after McCall left, a young man with dark hair entered the room pushing a wheelchair. "Hi, Teri," he said. "I'm Sean. I'm going to be your physical therapist. Are you ready to try to walk?"

"Oh, yes," I said. "I definitely am." Finally I could start returning to normal.

After helping me to sit up and removing all of the various medical devices from my limbs, Sean rolled the wheelchair over and prepared my portable oxygen and IV lines for the trip. "Okay. We're going to slowly help you get to a standing position. You can't use your arms to pull yourself up, only to steady yourself. Ready?"

I nodded. I'd stood up yesterday, and I could do it again. I needed to push through this in order to get back to my old self. Sean had me grab the wheelchair handles and start to stand.

Dizziness washed over me, and my body protested each movement. I could see the white specks in my vision that meant I was close to passing out. I came very close to saying it was too much, that I'd need to try again another time.

No! I could do this. Just ten seconds ago I'd committed to doing whatever it took, for my kids' sake. I couldn't back down on the first challenge. I steeled myself and stood up the rest of the way. Yes! I felt like I might collapse at any second, but I'd done it.

"Good," said Sean. "Now try rocking back and forth in place a bit, just shifting your weight from foot to foot."

That wasn't too hard. Maybe standing up was the worst of it.

"Okay. Now try to take a few steps forward."

I started to take the first step and nearly fell. *No way*, I thought. My legs weren't going to support me. The bed was right there, and I'd already accomplished standing up. That was probably enough for one day.

Then I thought about McCall, Jace, and Dallin again. The sooner I could walk, the sooner I could go home, and the sooner this would all be over. The thought cleared my head. I gritted my teeth, focused on the floor in front of me, and took a step forward.

I didn't collapse. I took another step. I was shaking and terrified that I was going to fall at any second, but I managed to do it.

"Can you do more?" asked Sean.

Now that I was in the midst of it, I decided to push my limits. "Yes."

We walked—slowly—out of the room. Every step felt like my feet were laden with bricks. Just a few steps out the door, I was exhausted. I felt dizzy and weak. *It's too hard. I can't possibly do it,* thought a voice in my head. *It's just too hard.*

Are you kidding me? answered another voice. *It's just walking!* What was wrong with me? I was an athlete. There was no way I was going to be beaten by a simple walk.

I started to think, as every part of my body screamed in pain and tears began to well up, *You have to do this. Just keep going.* I could do this. I *would* do this.

Taking one step at a time, we walked around the nurse's station before heading back to my room. It felt like an eternity. My therapist talked to me the whole time, trying to keep my mind off the pain. By the time I made it back to my bed, I wanted to just fall over, but a deep sense of triumph warmed my heart. I'd done it. Sean was very happy with my progress and told me he'd be back tomorrow.

As I started to fall asleep, I floated back to where I could see that beautiful place again. It looked different, farther away, and not as bright as before. I didn't know if I was leaving it, or if it was leaving me. I didn't know if I'd be able to return.

Maybe tomorrow would be better. Tomorrow's walk would be easier, for sure. There was no way it could be as hard as today. And maybe I'd be closer to the beautiful place again tomorrow, too. I just had to rest, and soon everything would be fine. Tomorrow I'd be closer to that place, and closer to my goal of going home.

5
MOVING FORWARD

Thursday, November 1

That day and the next, many people visited me, including some friends I hadn't seen in years. A nurse commented that she'd never seen so many people in the waiting room for just one person. Dallin, Jace, and McCall spent as much time with me as possible and talked constantly about the outpourings of love they were receiving every day. The flowers and gifts made them feel like they were family to all of the friends who showed their support. Tears filled my eyes as I thought about the blessings raining down on me and my kids. Dallin commented, "Heavenly Father knew we needed angels—lots of angels. And there they were, all around us."

McCall started bringing me a fruit smoothie every day, which felt wonderful on my throat.

Despite all the visitors, my room was mostly quiet, and I slept a lot.

Several different doctors checked on me, redoing my blood work, making sure my organs were healing properly. Everyone was amazed at my progress. One by one, the IVs and other things attached to my body came off. I could sit in the chair in my room, which was a great way to get out of the bed for a while.

I still found it hard to stand, walk, and even breathe deeply. I had to do special breathing exercises to build the strength back up in my lungs, which had been compromised during the two surgeries. Plus, even minor chest expansion hurt, so I needed to force myself to fully fill my lungs. I would blow into the breathing apparatus and try to keep the ball inside of it at a certain level, which always made me feel out of breath. *Really?* I thought. I was used to intensive cardio. And now I was having a problem with just breathing? Sure, everyone else was amazed by my progress, but it wasn't nearly fast enough for my tastes.

The more I healed, the more determined I became to push through my recovery quickly. I would do whatever it took for me to go home. I dreamed of sleeping in my own bed, as the hospital bed became less comfortable with each passing night. My back was a mess of knots, and the swelling throughout my body made it hard to sleep well. Seriously, with the amount of money those beds cost, you'd think they'd find a way to make them more comfortable.

They'd reduced my pain medication, and the residual anesthesia from the surgery was less and less present in my system. I didn't want to ask for more medication, since I didn't like the way it made me feel. The foggy-headedness made it hard to follow people's explanations of what I'd been through, and I wanted to understand the problem so that I could fix it. But oh, the nights were unbearable, filled with constant pain in my back, my chest, my tailbone, and everywhere else. I just knew if I could get home and sleep in my own bed, I'd find the comfort I was seeking. Everything would be okay once I was out of the hospital.

Dr. Schorlemmer came in again on Thursday afternoon, beaming as usual. "Good news. We're going to move you to a regular hospital room."

My mouth dropped open. "Really?"

"You're doing incredibly well—better than I ever imagined."

I was in shock. For days, everyone had been telling me it would be weeks and weeks before I could leave critical care. And now I was going to move to a regular hospital room? Wow!

The circulation boots on my legs came off. The catheter and the last IVs came out, except for one in one of my arms. My legs and feet still looked swollen, and of course my chest looked like a horror movie monster, but finally I was on my way to recovery.

I did have mixed feelings. I'd grown very close to my nurses in the ICU. They'd cared for me twenty-four seven since I arrived, doing an amazing job. I loved them with all my heart, and part of me didn't want to leave them. I was also scared. The ICU room was now empty of the hundreds of cords, lines, tubes, IVs, and all the equipment that initially surrounded me. Was I going to be okay without all of it? Was I rushing ahead too fast?

No, this was what I wanted. Everything would be fine. The sooner I went home, the better.

The time came. The ICU nurses on duty brought in a wheelchair. I was able to leave that hated bed and settle into the chair. As they pushed me out of the critical care unit, I said goodbye to my nurses—a bittersweet moment.

We passed several other rooms on the way out of the unit. Every patient in them looked close to death. A knot formed in my stomach. That was how I must've looked in the beginning. I owed my life to the incredible care

I received here. I couldn't waste that. I had to get back to my former self as soon as possible.

We arrived on the third floor. Workers were remodeling some of it, blocking off certain sections and making the whole area very noisy. We passed the nurses' station and wheeled into my new room.

It was small. Really small. I wasn't sure I liked it. It didn't have the endless rows of equipment that had filled my ICU room, so that was a plus. There was a bed, a chair, and...ooh! A bathroom with a door! I laughed at my own enthusiasm about that.

Transitioning from wheelchair to bed, I settled in. McCall happened to be there during the move, and I was grateful that I had someone familiar with me. My new nurses came in and introduced themselves—very sweet, adorable women. They explained that since I was off the IVs, I'd need to take my medications orally now, including pain meds. I needed to stay aware of my pain levels in order to learn how to manage the pain.

"Also, we'll be giving you a stool softener because you need to have a bowel movement."

"Wait. What? I've been here for almost two weeks and haven't pooped the entire time? Holy crap." I realized that was a pun, and we all laughed.

There were breathing exercises to be done, physical therapy sessions to complete, and I needed to start eating more. Et cetera, et cetera, et cetera. I started to feel overwhelmed. Just how much work was this recovery going to take?

Sean, my physical therapist, came in a bit later. "Are you ready for a walk?"

No, not really, I thought. I felt so weak and exhausted. I didn't want to walk; I wanted to sleep.

"Yes, I am," I answered. I figured if I said yes every time I wanted to say no, I'd speed up how quickly I could go home.

He showed me how to do something called a barrel roll in order to sit up. I had to lie down on my side and roll into a sitting position without using my arms. I managed it without too much difficulty, though I still trembled with pain when I first stood.

Then he put what looked like a leash around my waist. I flushed with humiliation. "A leash? Really?"

He shrugged. "Sorry. It's hospital procedure. If you start to fall, it'll help me catch you more quickly."

McCall came with us on the walk, and the strain of movement quickly put all embarrassment out of my head. My head spun with dizziness. My breath came short and shallow. My muscles shook.

"Are you okay?" Sean kept asking.

"Yes. I'm fine."

Oh my gosh, this was *so* hard. Every step I took meant another step I'd need to repeat in order to get back to my room. I pushed myself to keep going, even though inside I was panicking about the return trip.

"Mom, are you okay?" McCall asked.

"Yup. I'm good," I lied.

Pain, pain, pain, pain, pain. The walk around the nurses' station seemed like it would never end. I nearly screamed, "How much farther?" but I held it in and began shouting to myself in my head: *I have to do this. Just keep going, no matter how bad the pain feels. I can do this. I will do this.*

We finally made it back to my new room, and it seemed unfair that after all of that, it was also hard to get into the bed. I just wanted to collapse into it and fall asleep, but instead I had to move slowly and carefully to avoid damaging myself.

Okay. So the walk wasn't much easier than the first one. That was a setback. Still, I refused to believe that it could stay this difficult for much longer. I was out of the ICU, and that had to count for something. Things would definitely start to turn around now.

It occurred to me that I might be somewhat in denial, but I pushed that thought aside. If I was in denial, it was helping me, not hurting me. My recovery was progressing faster than anyone expected, and I was determined that it would keep doing so. Today, a regular hospital room. After that, home. It couldn't be long now before everything was back to normal.

6
STANDING SOLO

Of course McCall shared the amazing news with everyone, and a wave of people stopped by my hospital room now that they were able to visit. Flowers filled the room with their beauty and fragrances, and I regularly wept while reading cards from well-wishers. A small army had come to my family's rescue.

While I still didn't feel like eating much, I drank a lot of water. My bladder filled up quickly, so the next time a nurse came in to check my vitals, I said, "I think I need to get up and go to the bathroom."

"Good," she said. "Let's get you up."

I performed the barrel roll—ow—to lie on my side, and the nurse helped me to a sitting position. Already out of breath, I wondered how I was going to make it all the way to the bathroom. Maybe it was a good thing that my new room was so small. As the nurse helped me stand up, the gravity redoubled how full my bladder felt.

She helped me over to the bathroom, but I went in alone. I took care of business (I had to use a container to catch my urine so it could be checked, measured, and logged in), and realized I needed to stand back up.

The nurse was still waiting in my room. "Do you need help getting up?" she called.

"No, I can do it," I answered.

I took a deep breath. Placing my hands on my knees, I leaned forward and...stood up, just like that. I grinned. Yes! Finally something came easily.

As I washed my hands, I couldn't help but look at them. They didn't look like mine. Though the swelling had gone down, bruises still covered them, and they felt tender under the running water. *No*, I decided, *focus on the positive*. I'd used the bathroom on my own, and stood up without any help. The bruises would go away eventually. I just had to keep going.

The nurse let me sit in the room's chair for a while. It reclined a bit so that I could put my feet up. It felt good to sit upright, so she brought me the TV remote and some water.

"Could I have a Diet Coke?" I asked.

She checked my chart. "Yes, you can. At this point, it doesn't list any diet restrictions, which is awesome. It means your colon and kidneys are functioning normally." She brought me a cup of Diet Coke with a straw, as well as some crackers. I took a sip and smiled.

With just me alone in my room, I flipped through a few channels until I recognized a pair of people on the news. It was the daughter of one of my friends, being interviewed along with her husband. They'd been evacuated from their apartment due to Hurricane Sandy, and their area still had a lot of flooding and no power. They looked exhausted. So much devastation with so little warning. You never knew when a disaster would rip everything away.

McCall came in a few minutes later and brightened with excitement. "Wow, Mom, look at you! You look so good, and you're sitting up."

I held up my cup. "And I'm drinking a Diet Coke."

She laughed, but I could tell something important was on her mind. She practically bounced with excitement. "I just saw Dr. Schorlemmer. Guess what he told me?"

"What?"

She took a deep breath. "You could be going home this week."

If I wasn't so weak, I would have bolted upright. Earlier estimates had put me in the hospital for a lot longer than that. My kids had been told they'd be lucky to have me home by Christmas. "You're kidding. Really?"

"Yeah! I can't believe it. That's crazy, Mom!"

I was awestruck and thrilled by the news. Finally, my dreams of sleeping in my own bed, returning to my normal life, being at home where people wouldn't have to worry about me, could be realized.

McCall and I talked about that, and about the hurricane and other things happening in the world, before she dozed off in my bed. I could tell that she needed the rest. She looked exhausted.

A short while later, I realized I needed to pee again. I was about to call the nurse, but I didn't want to wake up McCall.

Since I was already sitting up, I decided I could take care of it myself. No need to bother anyone else. I'd stood up on my own earlier that day, so I knew I could do it again.

I placed my hands on my knees and slowly rose. So far so good. Moving carefully, I walked over to the bathroom, pleased at how I was able to move without assistance. After I finished, I shuffled my way back to the chair.

I must have made noise, because McCall looked up to see me standing there. "*What* are you doing, Mom?"

"It's okay," I said. "I just got up to go to the bathroom. I'm fine." For once, that was the truth.

She didn't look convinced. "Do you want me to call your nurse?"

"No, girl, really, I'm good." I smiled, and she relaxed.

She helped me climb back into the bed, and I enjoyed several other visitors throughout the evening, including Dallin and Jace. I still wasn't hungry for dinner, but the nurse helped me to the bathroom to brush my teeth. I was shaky, but I managed to brush for a few minutes before my arm became too tired. I avoided looking in the mirror. I didn't want to see the medical tape over the incision in my chest.

The nurse handed me a cup full of different medications, checked my vitals after I took them, and told me she wouldn't bother me for another four hours. Hopefully that meant I could sleep better than I did in the ICU, where they checked on me every hour. She left the bathroom light on and opened the bathroom door a bit in case I needed to use it. "You can do it on your own if you think you can, but please call me if you need any help." Shutting the room's door, she left me alone.

The room was much darker and quieter than my ICU room, but the bed wasn't any better. In fact, it might have been worse. I couldn't get comfortable. Every time I moved, I felt the strain and pain in my chest. Everything hurt. The light cast unpleasant shadows on the walls, and I felt flutters of anxiety, worries about what had happened and what might happen—possible complications from the surgery, a longer recovery time than I expected, the stress I'd brought on my kids. I didn't like the new room. I just wanted to go home.

It felt like no time at all before the nurse woke me up to check my vitals. "Hmm," she said. "Your heart rate and blood pressure are up a bit. Are you having trouble sleeping?"

"Yes," I admitted. "I just feel so uncomfortable." The pain worsened, and I added, "Actually, I feel like I've been hit by a truck."

"Well, what you've gone through is much worse than that," she said. "I'll put in a request for some sleeping medication tomorrow. Dr. Schorlemmer will probably prescribe something so you can rest." She made a note, then asked, "How is your pain level? You can have more pain medication if you'd like."

I considered her offer. Now that I was awake, my body was screaming again, and the medication sounded awfully tempting. Since I'd be asleep, I might not even be bothered by the fuzzy-headed feelings it brought on.

On the other hand, I didn't want to jeopardize my chances of going home soon, especially not after the good news McCall had shared with me. "No," I said. "I'll be fine."

The nurse frowned. "It's really okay for you to take the meds. Because you've had so much trauma, it's very important to keep your stress levels as low as possible. Pain causes a lot of stress, and your recovery process will go much smoother and faster if we can keep your pain to a minimum."

It was the middle of the night, and I desperately wanted to sleep. I wanted the pain to go away. I could admit defeat just this once. "Okay," I said. "Then it's probably a good idea for me to have some."

"Good choice," she said.

She brought me more meds in a cup, and it didn't take long for them to have an effect. The pain began to fade. I felt more comfortable than I had all day. Even the horrible bed didn't seem so bad.

I barely noticed my nurse doing another vitals check four hours later. She smiled at me. "Your vitals are much better. Go back to sleep."

The next thing I knew, it was morning. Breakfast carts rattled past my door, and hospital personnel walked by, carrying on conversations. I needed to use the bathroom again, but I didn't want to call for help. Not for something as simple as this. "I can do this," I told myself.

Breathing deeply, I rolled onto my side. The movement was graceless, but it hurt less than I'd expected. After a little pause to prepare, I rolled again to a sitting position and swung my legs over the side of the bed. I took another deep breath, placed my hands on my knees, and counted to three. One, two, three, go.

I stood up and wavered there for a second, surprised I'd been able to do it. Maybe moving out of the ICU had been good for me. I felt shaky, but the sense of triumph at getting out of the bed overshadowed any balance issues. After nine days of needing help for every little thing, I could finally move around again.

I finished in the bathroom and got myself back into bed before the nurses even came in for the morning. I shared my exciting news with them, and they looked thrilled. "They weren't kidding," one of them said. "We'd heard you were a miracle."

I smiled. This time, after my victory, the comment didn't feel so out of place.

After going over my medications and checking my vitals, they said they needed to weigh me again. I proudly climbed out of bed and positioned myself on the scale without help. As I looked down at the numbers, though, my sense of elation vanished.

165. After eating almost nothing, pushing myself as hard as I could in physical therapy, and finally managing to use the bathroom again, I still had thirty-five pounds of extra weight. How was that even possible?

The nurse cheerfully observed, "It looks like the water weight is slowly coming off."

Slowly was the right word. I looked at her, disappointed, and she tried to reassure me. "Don't worry. It will come off in no time."

Given how difficult every step of progress had been so far, it was hard to feel optimistic about that.

Her next comment, however, boosted my spirits right back up. "It looks like you might be going home soon. Dr. Schorlemmer will be here this morning. We'll see what he says."

Oh my gosh! I was thrilled. Sleeping in my own bed, living in my own house, wearing my own clothes…that was all I really wanted.

Since I could stand on my own, the nurse asked if I felt up to taking a shower. The thoughts of the warm water on my body sounded delightful. "I'd love to."

She taped up the IV line in my arm and told me it was okay for the incisions to get wet as long as we dried them thoroughly afterward. She helped me to the bathroom and untied the back of my hospital gown, and I sat down on the little bench in the shower.

The nurse washed my hair and massaged my head a bit, which felt exhilarating after so much time spent lying down on the hospital bed. Then she handed me a washcloth. "Take your time and wash yourself," she said. "If you're okay, I'll leave for a few minutes and be back to help you get out."

"I'm fine," I said. "If it's okay, I'd like to try and get myself out."

She smiled. "Sure. Once you're dry, pull the cord for the nurses' station, and I'll come in to dry your hair."

I'd planned on doing that myself, but I'd forgotten that I couldn't lift my arms yet. Oh, right. Debilitating injury.

At least I was making progress.

Warm water ran over my body, and for several minutes I just sat there and enjoyed the feeling. Eventually I picked up the washcloth to start scrubbing, and I caught sight of myself again. I didn't like what I saw. The blotchy colors and bruising. My leg with all of its incisions. My bloated stomach.

As I bathed, I discovered even more incisions that I hadn't noticed before. A four inch cut under my right collar bone. A three inch cut by my left bicep, looking like a goose egg. What were those for? Of course the enormous incision running down my chest was the worst. There were the three tube holes in my stomach and a wound in my groin area, too. Was this really my body now? It looked more like a Halloween costume than it looked like me.

I bent forward to let the water run down my aching back and closed my eyes so I didn't have to see any more. Why did this happen to me? I didn't understand. Alone with my body, I let go of some of the tight control I'd been keeping on my emotions. "Please, let this be a dream," I whispered. Tears poured out of my eyes and mingled with the shower water pooling in the drain. "Please just let this go away." Sobbing wracked my body, and with each movement, the incisions groaned in pain with me.

Crying exhausted me and made me start to feel shaky. Every wound throbbed, and I wanted to get back into bed. Not the torture-rack bed here, but my own bed at home—soft, gentle cushioning for my knotted-up spine. If I could just sleep comfortably, everything would be easier to deal with. Thinking of home made me cry even more.

Footsteps sounded outside the door. "How are you doing?" called the nurse. "Everything okay?"

How long had I been in there? "Yes," I whispered. I cleared my throat and answered more audibly. "Yes. I'm just enjoying the warm water. I'll get out soon."

"Okay. I'll be back in a couple minutes."

I washed the tears off my face and turned off the water. I had to be strong, both for my kids and myself. I didn't want to be mopey and depressed if they stopped by. Still sitting on the bench, I turned off the water and leaned forward to grab a towel from the sink. I dried my face and began gently drying my body, trying not to apply too much pressure. Blotting the incision on my chest required me to look at it, but I tried not to think about what I was doing. I was going to be fine. This was temporary. Once I made it home, everything would be fine.

I stood up and made it out of the shower without any help and stood in front of the sink. My nurse came in a few minutes later, and I sat on the side of the bed as she dried my hair. She also checked my incisions, helped me into a new gown, and brushed out my hair.

A little while after the nurse left, Dr. Schorlemmer came into my room, beaming as usual. "How's my miracle today?"

Despite my weepiness just moments before, I smiled. It seemed impossible not to smile at him. "I'm good. Just took a shower."

"Good." He went over my progress, which continued to astonish him. He looked thoughtful for a moment, then said, "I'm going to order a panel of blood work today. If I like the way everything looks, you might be able to go home tomorrow."

I couldn't possibly have heard right. "Tomorrow? Really?"

I was afraid he was going to change his mind or correct what he'd said, but he nodded. "Yes, tomorrow. It's pretty unbelievable. But I know you'll be more comfortable at home, and you'll be able to get more rest. We'll set up home healthcare, and you'll have to have someone with you twenty-four seven, but I think we can make that work."

My mind raced, and I couldn't pay attention to anything else he said after that. I could go home. I could go *home*.

This would be the turning point. After this, everything would be better. I was sure of it.

7
HOMEWARD BOUND

Sean arrived for my second physical therapy session of the day a few minutes later. He was barely in the door before I announced, "I'm going home tomorrow!"

"Really? That's awesome!" he exclaimed. We completed our usual walk (with me still on a leash) around the cardiac ward, and I felt lightheaded and drained as usual. When we arrived back at my room, though, Sean suggested, "Let's walk over to the cardiac rehab so you can see it. It's on this floor."

All I wanted to do was get back into bed, but I told him, "Sure, let's go." After all, pushing myself had worked so far.

By the time we walked out of the cardiac unit and into the waiting area, I regretted my decision. How much farther was it? We passed the elevators and headed into a completely different wing of the hospital. My mind screamed as my body lit up with pain, but I began my mantra: *I can do this. I have to do this. I WILL do this.*

I finally saw a sign on the wall for the cardiac rehab unit. Oh, yes! We were almost there.

Entering the rehab unit through a set of double doors, I saw what looked like a nice gym filled with well-maintained treadmills, stationary bikes, elliptical machines, and a weight area. Huge floor-to-ceiling windows ran along the whole length of the unit, facing the Wasatch Mountains. It was a fabulous view of the green and white peaks, and most of the equipment faced it, so I'd have something nice to look at while doing rehab.

Sean proceeded to point out various areas of the rehab unit. When I was ready, I would come in for cardiac therapy. There was a device that would electronically monitor my vitals as I began my road to recovery. "Normally heart patients are here within a week or two, but you probably won't come in for a month. Instead you'll have a therapist come to your home at first."

"Sounds great," I said. I was eager to begin getting back to normal, but at the moment I was worried about getting back to my room. My muscles were flagging, and dizziness swam through my head. As Sean began walking me back on the return trip, I had to lean on his arm in order to stay upright.

"Are you okay?" he asked.

"Yes, I'm just a little tired." *I will do this. I have to do this.*

McCall was waiting for us when we returned to the cardiac ward. She broke into a big smile when she saw me walking around. "Look at you!"

I wanted to run to her and take her in my arms, but of course I couldn't. Instead I clung to Sean as McCall walked up and hugged me. "Your nurses just told me you're coming home tomorrow. That's amazing!"

"I know, baby girl. I'm happy, too."

"Mom, are you okay?"

"Yeah, I just need to lie down."

Those last few steps into my room took everything I had. Sean and McCall helped me back into bed. I thanked Sean, and he left us alone.

McCall was still ecstatic. "Can you believe it? I'm so thankful you don't have to be here anymore. I know how much you wanted to come home." She squeezed my hand gently.

"I know it hasn't been easy on you and the boys, either. I'm so sorry for all I've put you through."

"Don't even say that. We don't care what it takes, we're just glad you're still here. I love you, and Dallin and Jace love you, and mom, so many people love you. You really have no idea how loved you are. All we need right now is for you to keep working to get better. You don't have to worry about us or anything else. Just focus on that."

Gratitude overwhelmed me. As I looked into her grown-up face, I could still see the day I found out I was pregnant with her.

***

It was in another hospital, and I'd gone in to have myself tested. Dallin was three and Jace was only eight months old. When I skipped a period, I couldn't believe I could be pregnant again. That only happened to careless people, and we had been careful. I immediately went into denial. Day after day, I continued to believe I wasn't pregnant. I had a toddler and an infant already. That was more than enough responsibility. When the reality finally set in that I was fifty-eight days late, I relented and decided to go to the local hospital for a pregnancy test. Still, I felt adamant that there was some other explanation. No way could I be pregnant again. No way.

The wait for the test results took forever, sitting in that hospital with baby Jace on my hip and fear in my heart. When a nurse finally came out and handed me my results on a folded sheet of paper, I couldn't bring myself to open it. I walked all the way out of the waiting room and into the elevator, looking at my beautiful baby boy, wondering how I could cope if I had another child now. The elevator began its descent, and I finally mustered the courage to open the paper.

It read positive. '

Tears filled my eyes, and I blinked several times, hoping the results would change. *Please no. Please no. This just can't be right.*

The results stayed the same.

As I drove home, sobbing, I was suddenly hit with a strong feeling that this baby must have a very important reason to come into our family at that time. There was a greater purpose behind the timing.

I didn't know it then, but she would literally save my life.

***

Looking at her now at nineteen, so responsible and mature for her age, I was never more grateful for her. I had always felt blessed by her presence in my life, but I could now see her hidden reserves of strength and the depths of love she felt for me. I was overcome with emotion, and just squeezed her hand.

We both fell asleep, me in my bed and her in the chair, until the nurse brought in my lunch. Nothing looked appetizing, but McCall took a short trip to get me a fruit smoothie, easily the highlight of the day. While she was gone, I noticed she'd brought my iPad in and left it on the table beside me. I decided to see what she had posted on Facebook, so I logged in and began scrolling through the responses.

I was shocked by how many comments there were from friends and family, praying for my recovery, offering help to my kids, or just expressing their support. This was all for me? Really? I couldn't get through them all, and I cried through those that I did manage to read. There were so many.

Dallin and Jace stopped by while I was reading, and they, too, couldn't believe I was going home tomorrow. They both looked drained, and I knew they were exhausted from trying to juggle this crisis with work and school. Like McCall, they were being pushed to their limits and doing their best to stay strong. I couldn't wait to be at home, where it would be easier for them to spend time with me, and I could sleep more soundly and finally stop feeling like an invalid.

***

Friday, November 2

Morning came. I woke up in a rush of excitement—today was the big day. As I lay there, I felt some weird movements in my stomach. I couldn't place what they were at first, until I remembered the nurse saying I had to have a bowel movement before I could leave. Well, no time like the present.

I was worried it was going to hurt, but my colon was apparently working properly. Everything went well. No big deal. One step closer to going home.

After I was finished, I didn't want to get back into bed. Though it hurt to stand, I walked over to look out the window. The sun was shining beautifully. The people outside wore jackets and coats, so it was probably cold. I remembered it had been rainy the night I went to the ER. How long ago was that? Two weeks? It felt much longer. Today I'd get to go outside again for the first time since that night.

I couldn't stand the idea of climbing back into that bed, so instead I sat in the chair. It was time for a shift change, so my regular nurse came in to introduce me to the nurse who'd be on duty until I went home. The new nurse smiled at me. "I've heard all about you. You are quite a miracle."

I smiled. "That's what I'm told." They checked my vitals and outlined what would happen before I left the hospital, and then breakfast arrived. I managed to try the scrambled eggs and a few bites of toast, but the fruit and yogurt were still the best part.

Shortly afterward, Dr. Schorlemmer came in. "Hey, miracle girl! Are you ready to go home today?"

"Yes, sir, I am." I said, grinning. I could already tell by his demeanor that he had good news.

"Well, your blood work looks great. Your progress continues to be amazing. Everything seems good, so once the paperwork has been processed, you'll be able to leave. It should only be an hour or two. After that, I'll see you in my office in two weeks."

Tears of joy welled up in my eyes. "Thank you, thank you so much." Despite how hard it still was to move, I slowly pushed myself out of the chair and walked over to give him a hug. "Thank you for saving my life."

He returned the hug. "You've survived what few survive. Thank you for fighting so hard."

Seconds after he left, I was on the phone with McCall. "I'm coming home!"

She squealed with happiness. "I'll bring you some clothes! Is there anything else you need?"

"No, that's it." I realized I was still bloated, so I added, "Just be sure to find the biggest pair of sweats I have. They're probably the only thing I can fit into."

Sean arrived to take me for one last walk. As we completed our usual route around the floor, he asked, "Do you have stairs in your house?"

"Yes. It's a townhouse. My bedroom is on the second floor."

He nodded. "Would you like to try some stairs before you go home?"

I knew I'd promised myself that I would accept every challenge, but at this point I was so drained from the regular walk that I really didn't want to do any more. Besides, I'd probably have to do a lot of moving around as I returned home, and I didn't want to tire myself out. "No, it's okay," I decided.

"Are you sure?"

"Yeah. I'll be fine. The stairs shouldn't be a big deal."

He walked me back to my room and said he'd see me in a few weeks when I started rehab.

McCall burst in a few moments later. "Mom, you're coming home! I can't believe it!" I think if I was healthy, we would have grabbed each other and jumped up and down. "Lindsi and Larissa came and cleaned the house yesterday," McCall continued. "And I organized your closet, so now it doesn't look like it belongs to a hoarder."

I laughed. "Thank you, sweetie. That was nice of Lindsi and Larissa. They didn't have to do that."

"I know. But they really wanted to. Oh, and Lindsi and Alba brought you a present—a bench seat for your shower."

"Ooh, I'll need one of those. That's so nice of them!" I felt a little ridiculous to be so excited about a shower seat, but my optimism was too strong to fight.

In anticipation of the big moment, McCall helped me to get dressed. "Beware," I warned her as she untied my hospital gown. "I look pretty scary."

"Mom, you're beautiful. Nothing can change that."

I steadied myself on the chair as she helped me put my legs into the sweats. It took all the effort I had to lift my foot a couple of inches, and even that much movement sent lances of fire shooting up my leg. My body shook, and I gripped the back of the chair until my knuckles turned white. Ow, ow, ow, ow. We finally got both feet in. McCall pulled the sweats up over me, and I looked down at them. "They're snug."

"Just a little."

"They're usually three sizes too big."

"Don't worry about it, Mom. You'll be back to your normal shape soon."

Next she pulled a t-shirt over my head and slowly maneuvered my arms through the arm holes. My chest felt tight, and when she finished, the neck of the shirt rested on my incision, which was uncomfortable, but didn't quite hurt. I could live with it. She brushed out my hair and put it in a messy bun on top of my head. I brushed my teeth, and then I was ready to go.

I was also exhausted. McCall helped me sit back down in the chair, and I dozed off while she channel surfed.

My nurse returned to give me the instructions for my home healthcare. A *lot* of instructions. Fortunately, McCall focused, took notes, and asked clarifying questions, so at least she knew what was going on. They went over my medications, dosages, and my scheduled appointment with Dr. Schorlemmer in ten days. The nurse also made sure we had all of the phone numbers we needed.

When the meeting was over, she left to get a wheelchair. McCall packed up the few belongings I had with me, as well as the one remaining flower arrangement to bring home. They helped me sit down in the wheelchair, put flip-flops on my swollen feet, and wheeled me out of that room for the last time. I waved goodbye as we passed the nurses' station. The nurses met me with cries of "good luck," "best wishes," "you'll do great" and so on.

Every foot covered was another foot closer to home. The rhythm of the wheels on the floor began another rhythm in my mind: *I'm going home! I'm going home! I'm going home!*

It wasn't until we reached the elevator that my nerves kicked in. What if I wasn't ready? What if this was too fast? Could I handle it?

No, I was being silly. The move out of ICU had been fine, and this would be fine, too. I just needed to get home, and then everything would be better.

As we passed through the huge revolving doors, a rush of chilly air took my breath away. I gasped.

"You okay, Mom?" McCall asked.

"Yes, I'm fine." Once the initial shock was over, the fresh air in my lungs and the sun on my skin both felt wonderful.

The valet came around to help me get into the car as McCall loaded my stuff into the trunk. Together they helped me stand up and make my way into the passenger seat. I shivered from the cold, eager for them to shut the door so we could be on our way.

McCall snapped the seatbelt into place, and I gasped again, this time in pain. "It's too much pressure on my chest," I panted. "It's too much. I can't stand it."

She hurried to pull the belt away from my incisions and tucked it under my arm instead. "Is that better?"

"Yes, much." I sighed with relief. If that was the biggest problem I faced today, I'd be a happy woman.

The valet closed the door, McCall hopped into the driver's seat, and I took a deep breath.

"Ready?" McCall asked.

"Absolutely. Let's go."

Little did I know at the time how hard the journey ahead of me was going to be. It would be long, both mentally and physically. I still didn't understand the magnitude of what had happened to me. I hadn't asked many questions about my condition. I didn't want to know the details. Despite everyone telling me how miraculous I was and how lucky I was to be alive and how long it would take to recover, I reasoned that if I was doing so well already, I could keep pushing my limits until I was back to my old self. Sure, my aorta had torn, but how big a deal could that be? Three or four weeks, and I'd be back to work and back to my normal life. After Thanksgiving, probably, or after Christmas at the latest. Going home was just the first step in the race back toward health. And I was a sprinter. I intended to sprint the rest of the way.

8
THE STAIRS

It felt strange to sit in the same car that took me to the emergency room less than two weeks ago. The weather during the first ride felt like fall. Now it seemed that winter was just around the corner. The first ride was full of anxiety, sleepiness, and annoyance. I expected the second ride to be filled with excitement, relief, and determination.

It was, for about ten seconds. Physical discomfort quickly overshadowed my emotions Even the vibrations of the car made my injuries ache, and the slightest bump made me cringe. My hands clenched around the armrests until my knuckles turned white, and I forced myself to keep breathing. I started to lose feeling in my head.

Was I really so weakened? I didn't feel like myself, and I certainly didn't look like myself. It scared me to think how quickly life could take this kind of turn.

McCall noticed that I was in pain. "Mom, I'm sorry, I know the bumps aren't helping. Is there anything I can do?"

"Just keep driving, baby girl," I said. "I just need to get home." In just a few minutes, I'd lie down in my own bed, and everything would be fine.

"Do you want to listen to some music? Maybe it'll help distract you," said McCall.

I wasn't sure that would work, but it was worth a try. "Sure."

She turned on the radio, and my head tried to explode. The sound was just too much. "Turn it off!" I managed to say.

McCall switched the radio back off, and I tried to calm down. My chest was on fire, and I started to panic. How much longer would this take? How much longer would I have to sit in this awful seat and endure the horrible seatbelt across my body? As I looked out the window, trying to get my mind off the pain, I saw people everywhere, out and about, living their lives. It was just an ordinary day. Life had not come to a complete stop for anyone but me. Why did this happen to me? I didn't want to upset McCall, but tears pooled in my eyes anyway. For the first time, I felt truly afraid.

You need to relax, I told myself. I wanted to freak out, but I couldn't do that to McCall. I could tell she was anxious. I remembered to take deep breaths. Breathe in, breathe out.

"Don't worry," I said. "I'm fine. Just a little overwhelmed."

I didn't think she believed me.

After twenty minutes—though it felt like twenty years—we finally turned onto our street. I noticed how adorable our neighborhood looked, with its lovely houses and cheery-looking rooms visible through front windows. You could tell it was a neighborhood of homes, not just residences. It felt like ages since I'd been there. The Halloween decorations were still up, and I realized my sense of time felt way off. I couldn't remember if we'd passed the holiday already or not.

"Did I miss Halloween?" I asked McCall.

"Yes, that was two days ago." McCall pulled into the driveway, and I saw a huge sign across the front of the garage: *WELCOME HOME, MOM!*

Despite the pain, I couldn't help but smile.

We pulled into the garage, and McCall came around the car to help me out. My body was shaking after the car ride, but with my daughter steadying me I managed to climb out of the car and walk slowly toward the door. Three steps led into the house, but by this point I just wanted to get inside. We took them one at a time, pausing after each one, and I sighed with relief as I finally made it indoors. I'd missed being here. The kitchen and eating area beckoned to me, so warm and inviting. The family room, with the fireplace so cozy, promised relaxing nights of curling up with a cup of tea and a good book. I breathed in deeply, enjoying the scent of my own home instead of the antiseptic of the hospital. I was home. I was really home. It had only been about ten days, but it felt like I hadn't been there in forever, like I was returning to a different life. I'd worried that nothing would ever be the same again, but now that I was home, I thought everything would be okay. Now I could finally start to relax.

As McCall helped me into the kitchen, I saw the kitchen counter crammed with food, snacks, and treats. I looked at McCall in confusion. "Did someone run to the grocery store right before we arrived?"

She laughed. "I know, right? So many people are bringing us food. We're definitely not going to go hungry."

Realizing the food and snacks were gifts from our friends, I again felt overwhelmed. So many people stepped up to look out for my kids while I was in the hospital. I'd never be able to thank them enough.

"Can we go up to my room?" I asked. "I'm pretty tired."

"Of course," said McCall. She knelt down and slipped my flip-flops off my feet. "It might be easier without them."

With her stabilizing me, I walked slowly out of the kitchen toward the stairs. *Okay,* I thought, *this is it. Just climb these stairs, and you can sleep in your own bed. Piece of cake.*

I grabbed the handrail. McCall held me up on the other side. I slowly, carefully lifted my foot.

We climbed the first step. So far so good.

We climbed the second step. My legs started to shake.

Third step. I must've looked nervous, because McCall began encouraging me. "You can do this, Mom. You're doing great."

Fourth step. My heart raced. My fingers tightened on the handrail and on McCall's arm, which made the pain in my chest flare up even more.

Fifth step. Lifting my leg took almost all of my energy. I leaned forward to catch my breath. My head spun.

Sixth step. I wasn't even sure how I made it up that one. I struggled to keep it together, but tears threatened the corners of my eyes.

Seventh step. Every part of my body screamed for me to stop. Sweat poured down my back, and I hunched over against the pain in my chest, trying to remember to keep breathing. I wanted to quit, but that was no longer an option. Going back down would take even longer. I had to do this. I had to finish.

I fixed my eyes on the last step to the landing, struggling to block out enough of the pain to force myself to climb up.

Eighth step.

It took everything I had left in me, but we made it to the landing.

We were halfway done.

I broke down completely. "McCall," I cried, "I can't do this! I can't do this! I can't do this!" The tears pooling in my eyes spilled over, and I wept uncontrollably, bent over, wanting to clutch my arms against the burning pain, but not sure which ache needed soothing the most. "Why is this so hard?" I wailed. "Why? Why?"

McCall's eyes filled with panic as I lost it. "Mom, the boys aren't home. Should I call someone for help?"

"Why?" I cried. My voice rose to a hysterical pitch. "Why, why, why is this so hard? I shouldn't have come home from the hospital. I can't do this. How am I going to do this?"

McCall looked around with huge eyes as if she hoped someone would pop out of a closet to help, and I realized she was terrified. I forced myself to take a deep breath before I could start hyperventilating. Losing control wouldn't make this any easier. I needed to focus. I needed to stay in control for my daughter's sake.

I was only halfway up the stairs. There were eight behind me and eight in front of me. I had to choose one of them to conquer. There was no other option—not unless I wanted to stay on the landing for the rest of my life.

I looked at the stairs ahead of me and swallowed, remembering to breathe. I'd climbed half of them. I could climb the other half. They would not beat me.

I took a shuddering breath. "No," I told McCall. "Don't call anyone. I can do this." She gave me a disbelieving look, and I repeated my mantra from the hospital. "Really. I can do this. I have to do it."

Eyes still the size of dinner plates, she nodded. "Okay. Here we go."

Deep breath in. Deep breath out. Deep breath in.

First step.

***

After an excruciating eternity, we made it to the top of the second half of the stairs. I bent forward and took deep breaths. I wanted to collapse. My clothes were soaked with sweat, my limbs shook, and my head swam with dizziness. I never, ever wanted to do that again.

But I made it.

McCall beamed at me, and I could see the relief in her face. "Awesome, Mom, you did it!"

I tried to smile back at her and give her my usual sassy response, but it came out in a wheeze. "Told you I could."

She took my arm again, and I leaned heavily on her as we headed down the hall toward my room.

As we entered the room, I looked at my bed, desperate to climb up into it, curl up in a ball, and go to sleep for a very long time. As I stood next to it, I discovered a problem.

The bed was too high.

At that point I was too tired to care, and instead I pointed toward the loveseat, which seemed to beckon me with its low, easily accessible cushioned surface. "I don't think I can get into my bed," I told McCall. "I'll just sleep on the couch."

She helped ease me down onto the loveseat and lifted my legs up on the ottoman. As she adjusted the pillows to make me comfortable, I lay my pounding head back and tried to forget about the ordeal on the stairs. Nothing had ever been that hard. Absolutely nothing. I hadn't thought I could survive that kind of pain.

McCall finished situating the couch and asked, "Are you hungry?"

"No," I said. "Maybe just some water."

"Okay. I'll be right back."

I heard her leave the room and head back down the stairs to the kitchen:

eight, seven, six, five, four, three, two, one, done. Just like that.

How could something so simple be so hard? What was wrong with me?

I opened my eyes and looked around the room, grateful to at least be home. I noticed several different little posters hung around the room, all in McCall's writing: *We missed you! You are the best! We love you!*

I smiled. That was sweet.

My room was full of beautiful floral arrangements, which had been sent throughout my hospital stay. I wanted to look at them all and read all of the posters, but my eyes closed of their own accord. I quickly fell into a deep sleep.

9

BED, BATH, AND BODY IRKS

A soft voice woke me. "Mom? I know you're tired, but you need to wake up. You need to eat something and take your meds."

I opened my eyes to see McCall leaning over me. Why was McCall giving me meds instead of one of the nurses? And where *were* the nurses? And why didn't the room smell or feel like a hospital?

I blinked the bleariness out of my eyes and looked around. Oh, that's right, I was home! An enormous grin spread across my face. This wasn't a dream. This was reality.

I looked up at McCall. "Okay, girl. I'll try."

While McCall moved to get my meds ready, another relative, Aunt Janice, came in to see me. She had the same kind of weariness in her expression as McCall, but I could see the love and concern on her face. "Hey, Teri. How are you doing?"

"I'm good," I said, as usual. Maybe if I said it enough times, it would come true. "What are you doing here?"

McCall spoke from across the room. "Janice and Dick are going to stay with you for a few hours, remember?"

I thought back over the conversations from the past few days. Oh, yes, a good friend of mine had invited my kids to go to Cirque Du Soleil, wanting to take them to do something fun in the midst of all the craziness. They'd all thought I'd still be in the hospital at this point, so it was nice of Janice and Dick to keep an eye on me while the kids had a much-deserved break.

Hearing our voices, Jace and Dallin came in. "Hey, Mom!" they each said. They took turns gently hugging me and giving my cheek a kiss.

It was almost a party in my room for a few minutes as we all hung out. McCall busied herself organizing my meds, making signs to remind me and my visitors of what I could and couldn't do—no lifting, no reaching, don't pull on her arms when you help her move, no bending down, no excitement—and generally getting things ready for the day. When she finished with that, she helped me up and into the bathroom as the other guests headed back downstairs.

I sat down on the toilet, doing my best to ignore the pain all across my body, and caught a glimpse of myself in the mirror. I still looked awful. My chest chose that moment to send a wave of agony lurching through my torso, and I bent double against it. "What happened to me?" I gasped to McCall. "I can't do this. This isn't me."

"Mom, don't cry," McCall said in a soothing tone. "Everything is going to be okay. You *can* do this." She ran back into my bedroom and returned holding a pair of new pajamas. "I bought you some cozy, warm PJs. The top buttons up, so it'll be easy for you to get them on and off." She then pulled over my office chair, which she'd apparently placed in the bathroom. "I also brought this in to give you somewhere to sit. You're going to get through this, Mom. You can do this."

She helped me switch to a sitting position in the chair. I looked up at her, marveling at how strong she was trying to be for me. I had to do the same for her. "I know," I said. "You're right. Everything will be fine." I wasn't sure I believed it anymore, but I needed to make myself believe it for her and the boys.

She gave me my meds and helped me change out of my clothes and into my new pajamas. Every movement brought a different kind of pain to my body, but it was nowhere near as bad as the stairs from the day before. I avoided looking at my bare chest in the mirror. I didn't want to see the huge incision again.

When I finished changing, I discovered that the pajama bottoms were snug, despite having an elastic waist.

McCall noticed, too. "Maybe I should have bought a bigger size."

"Ugh," I groaned. "I'm fat."

"Mom, it's just water weight. It'll be gone before you know it."

"That's what they said at the hospital, but it's still here. I feel ugly. This whole recovery is taking too long."

"Well, you've been through a lot."

I sighed. "I know, I know. I just wish that the little things were easier."

McCall patted my shoulder. "Let me fix your hair. That'll help."

She did my hair, which did indeed make me feel a bit better. Then she asked me a very difficult question. "Do you want to go downstairs?"

Oh boy.

I *wanted* to go downstairs. That was where everyone would be, and I didn't want to stay in one room all day. If I was going to do that, I might as well have stayed in the hospital. But the agony of climbing the steps yesterday still burned fresh in my memory. If I went down, would I be able to come back up again?

McCall must have picked up on my line of thought. "If you do go downstairs, we can help you back up when we get home. Both Jace and Uncle Dick will be here to help steady you."

The promise of having two strong guys to catch me if I passed out from the pain was a comfort. I remembered my determination to rise against any challenge. Earlier today was just a fluke, I told myself. I was tired. I'd just come home from the hospital. The stairs would be easier the second time around. I paused for a moment to double-check my decision and then nodded. "Okay. I can do it. Let's go downstairs."

My breath came hard and fast as we walked to the top of the stairs. I was scared, but I'd committed to this, and I wanted to follow through. I held the handrail on one side as Dallin came up to steady me on the other side. Deep breath in. Deep breath out. Deep breath in.

First step.

And...wow. It was so much easier.

Yes, each movement still hurt. Yes, I still moved at a snail's pace. Yes, it was still embarrassing to have so much trouble with such a simple task. But the agonizing torture of the day before was lessened to regular pain. Maybe I was right. Maybe it really was just a fluke yesterday.

Or maybe it was easier to go down than up. I wouldn't know until later. For the moment, I kept a positive mindset.

Aunt Janice met us at the bottom and helped me sit at the kitchen table. Laura, a friend from work, arrived a few minutes later to visit me. "Hey Fruitloop," she said. "Glad to see you're up." She walked over, gave me a gentle hug, and pulled up a chair. "How are you feeling?"

"I'm good," I said. While it might not be objectively true, I did feel pretty happy about the relative ease of the trip down the stairs.

McCall brought me a bowl of soup and a plate with some other food. Everything smelled delicious—real food was like a dream after all of that hospital food. Unfortunately I wasn't terribly hungry, but I did manage a few bites.

McCall and Jace headed out to the show, and Dallin left shortly afterward. The rest of us settled on the couch to watch the Jazz game. Aunt Janice got particularly into it. She'd held season tickets for the last twenty years, and her mood varied throughout basketball season depending on how the team was doing. It was fun listening to her enthusiasm as the game progressed. The soft leather of the couch felt very comfortable, and for a short time, my injuries seemed to fade.

It couldn't last forever. It seemed that every time I held a position for more than five minutes, all sense of comfort fled. My chest began to feel heavy, and the incision ached. Breathing became strenuous, and I had to concentrate on each breath. I looked around the room to see if anyone had noticed, not wanting to disrupt the game or cause them to worry. Maybe if I ignored it, it would pass.

It did not pass. I stuck it out for a few more minutes, but finally I couldn't stand it any longer. I announced, "I think I'm ready for bed." At least that was a low-stress way of phrasing my needs.

Everyone scrambled to help me, and I felt guilty for grabbing all of the attention. *It's okay,* I thought. *I'll just climb the stairs and get into bed, and then they can all relax again.* It hadn't been too bad coming down, so hopefully that meant it would be easier going up.

Uncle Dick helped me to the bottom of the stairs. I felt weak already, and all I wanted to do was get into bed and sleep. Only the stairs stood in my way.

I. Can. Do. This.

We began. Uncle Dick put a gentle, but steady grip on my right hand. I held the railing with my left. Janice and Laura walked behind us in case I fell.

First step.

Oh. Oh no. Oh no, no, no.

This was not going to be easier.

Every step felt like sharp, hot pokers jabbed into my body. My eyes watered, but I was squeezing them shut so hard against the pain that no tears could actually fall. I panted for breath and felt sweat running down my body.

Somehow, after an eternity, we made it to the top. We had to pause so that I could catch my breath and regroup. I could see my bedroom door down the hall. All I wanted to do was to curl up and sleep.

"Do you want to brush your teeth?" asked one of my helpers as we shuffled to the bedroom.

I shook my head, which didn't help the way it was spinning.

This time, I had enough assistants that I was able to climb up into my bed. They helped me sit on the edge, and then they lifted my legs up and turned me so that I could lie down. They propped some pillows up behind my torso, and I sighed, anticipating relief, as I sank back against them.

Ughhh! Would *nothing* ever be easy again? The second I let my body rest against the pillows, pressure lit up across my chest, and I had to bite my lip to keep from screaming in surprise and frustration. This was not fair.

"I need more pillows behind me," I gasped, feeling an anxiety attack rising.

Janice and Dick both looked panicked, and they helped Laura to place more pillows behind me, adjusting my position so that I was sitting mostly upright. The pain in my chest lessened, though it didn't go away completely.

I took several shaky breaths. Okay. I was in bed, and I no longer felt like

I was dying. This was progress. I took stock of my body, hoping the remaining pain would fade away and I could finally go to sleep.

They pulled a blanket over me and asked, "How's that?"

"Good," I said before I thought about it. A few seconds later, I realized it wasn't good at all. The bed felt hard as a rock, not like the cushiony paradise I fantasized about at the hospital. Having my legs stretched out in front of me hurt them and put pressure on my chest, but I didn't have the strength to bend them up beside me, and I knew without trying that I wouldn't be able to sleep on my side anyway. "Maybe some pillows under my knees?" I asked.

Immediately my brigade of helpers obliged. The extra pillows relieved some of the pain, and I decided that was enough. I wanted everyone to leave. I wanted to sleep. And darn it, pain or no pain, I wanted to sleep in my bed. "Thanks," I said. "I'm good."

Not one of them looked convinced. "Really," I repeated. "I'm fine."

"Okay," said Laura, "if you're sure." She bent to give me a hug. "I'm heading home. I know you need to rest. I'll check on you tomorrow. Love you."

"Love you too," I said. "I really appreciate all you guys have done."

They each responded with a variation of "you're worth it," which brought a smile to my face. The trio headed downstairs (eight, seven, six, five, four, three, two, one, done), and I heard Laura leave through the front door to go home.

Right afterward, McCall and Jace returned home. They came up to see me, since I was still awake.

"Wow, you're tucked in there!" McCall said. She grinned. She'd heard me sing the praises of my own bed while I was in the hospital.

"How does it feel?" asked Jace.

"Great," I said. Well, lied.

They told me about the show, and I tried to be pleasant, but I was feeling more and more like I couldn't stay where I was. It was like the bed itself was fighting me, trying to evict me and force me back to the impersonal couch. The more it fought, the more I tried to fight back, forcing myself to breathe and ignore the aches and pains and strains creeping throughout my body.

I kept it together throughout the conversation, and finally Jace headed downstairs to check out the highlights of the Jazz game with Janice and Dick.

McCall hesitated. "Mom, are you really okay?"

Yet another wave of pain wracked my chest. I gave in. "No," I admitted. "I need to get out of this bed." Defeated and miserable, I started to cry. How was it possible that my own bed was even worse than those horrid beds at the hospital? It was supposed to be a comfort, a place I could relax.

It felt more like a torture rack.

McCall helped me sit up and slide off the bed. I watched the ground as we walked over to the loveseat, only half-hearing her reassurances and expressions of sympathy. She situated me on the couch and propped me up with pillows, then did the same with my arms to relieve the pressure on my chest, and with my legs to relieve the strain on them. Lastly, she covered me with a blanket.

"How's that?" she asked.

Physically, I felt much better. This was actually pretty comfortable.

Emotionally, I felt awful. First the stairs, now the bed. My home, supposed to be my sanctuary, was actually my enemy. It wouldn't surprise me if my toothbrush started causing me pain next.

"I'm okay," I said.

She brought me my evening meds, and after taking them I tried to settle down to sleep. McCall decided to sleep in my room in case I needed help.

"Wake me up if you need anything," she said. "I love you."

"Okay," I said, already drifting as that floating feeling overtook me. "Love you too."

The beautiful place appeared in front of me, the farthest away it had ever been. I reached for it, wanting nothing more than to return there. I wanted it back. Nothing in the real world was what I'd expected. I needed that feeling of peace and calm that came with the beautiful place. It began to grow closer, and for a second my hopes rose, but then it rushed past me in a whirlwind, too fast for me to grab it and force it to stay.

Then it was gone.

My mind began a scattered journey, jumping from one place to another to another, never stopping long enough for me to make sense of what was going on. Where was I? What was I doing? How did I get here? How could I get back to where I was supposed to be?

In the middle of the chaos, one solid concept intruded: McCall's voice. "Are you okay?"

I latched onto that reality. I didn't know what else was happening, but I knew my daughter. I knew my sons. They were here, and I could cling to that.

McCall spoke again. "Mom, are you okay?"

I opened my eyes to see her sitting up in bed. My mouth felt dry and sore, and I had to clear my throat a couple times before I could speak. "Sorry. Did I wake you up?" I asked.

"You were talking," she said. "Saying things I couldn't understand."

I blushed. "Sorry. I think I was having some crazy dreams."

"It's okay," she said. "I'm just glad you're all right."

She helped me use the bathroom and brought me a drink of water, and then we both went back to sleep. I dozed on and off, fighting phantasms in my mind, struggling to find a place where I could just rest. No such place existed. I finally opened my eyes in the dark bedroom, unwilling to keep up the fight.

Every part of my body ached. I glanced over and saw that McCall was still asleep. I didn't want to wake her. There wasn't anything she'd be able to do for my discomfort, and I knew she needed rest. So I sat there in the dark, wondering when morning would come and provide me with some distraction from my troubled body and my troubled mind.

After an uncertain amount of time, I dozed off. More agitating dreams. More physical pain. I woke up. It was still dark.

Would this nightmare never end?

10
NIGHTFALL

Saturday, November 3

After multiple spurts of restless sleep, punctuated by waking up in the darkness, I finally fell asleep again. This time, when I woke, it was light outside. Thank goodness, the night was over.

My entire body felt stiff. I tried to adjust my position, with little success. My movements woke McCall. "You okay, Mom?" she asked.

"Yes, I'm fine. I just need to change my position. Maybe sit up a little more. My back is so sore."

"Well, your home healthcare nurse is coming today. Do you want to shower before that?"

Ooh. Yes. A shower would feel so good. I could already imagine the warm water running over my stiff muscles and working out their tension.

McCall helped me to undress and sit on the bench seat, which she had installed the previous day. She adjusted the water so that it flowed over me, and I felt the rush of warmth as it ran down my body. Some of the night's anxiety started to fade.

The stream of water hit the incision on my chest, and the sensation made me lose my breath. I instinctively put up my hand to shield my chest from the water, and instead bent down to let it run across my back. That felt so good. I wanted to stay there forever.

McCall washed my hair, and then handed me my washcloth. As I bathed, I again took an inventory of my many incisions, bruises, and swollen areas. I discovered even more that I hadn't noticed in the hospital.

My relief from the shower began to fade. I felt trapped by this monstrosity that was now my body. How could this be me? I couldn't climb stairs. I couldn't sleep in a bed. I couldn't even wash my own hair. What good was I anymore?

McCall helped me to dry off and then dress in another new pair of pajamas. There was another thing to add to the list of problems: It was the start of the day, and I could only dress in sleepwear. I felt beaten down and almost wished I hadn't gotten out of bed, except that I knew that staying in one position all day would be intolerable. I just couldn't win.

I managed an unsettled sleep on the couch for about an hour before my home healthcare nurse arrived. I didn't think I could handle the stairs again, so she came up to my room instead.

"Hi," she said. "My name is Ruth." She sat down on the couch next to me and pulled out some paperwork. "Do you know how lucky you are to be alive? I've never seen anyone survive something like this."

"Yeah, so many people tell me that," I said. I was growing sick of hearing the same thing. If I was so miraculous, why did I still feel so broken?

Ruth explained that she and another nurse would come to see me three or four times a week, coordinating everything with Dr. Schorlemmer. She checked my vitals and incisions, told me to look out for various warning signs of infection, went over my many, many medications, and then explained the basics of my care to McCall.

I didn't want to hear all of this, so I trusted that McCall would remember it. However, one instruction stuck in my mind: "Make sure that Teri has someone with her twenty-four seven."

Really? I couldn't even be left alone? What was I, a child? Or some kind of invalid? I was an athlete, a sprinter, a healthy adult. To be so helpless that I literally couldn't do anything for myself was maddening and humiliating.

Once Ruth left, promising to return the following Monday, I managed to doze off again, despite feeling uncomfortable in my position on the couch. Strange things floated through my mind—spiders crawling around me in the shadows, just out of sight, too hard to catch. Creepy, spindly things grabbed at me out of the darkness, and I ran from them, but couldn't escape. One of them wrapped around my leg, and I tripped, but instead of hitting the ground, I kept falling, falling, falling off a cliff. There was no telling when I would hit the bottom.

My body jerked, and I woke up in a cold sweat, breathing heavily. It was just a bad dream, I told myself. Just a bad dream.

If only it was all just a bad dream.

Visitors streamed through the house throughout the day, though none of them stayed too long. In between guests, I tried to sleep again, but my mind wouldn't let me rest. The spiders and monsters lurked in the dark corners, tormenting my unconscious mind, waiting to grab me and drag me off into the abyss with them. I fought them off, but I could feel myself growing weaker. My back ached from my position on the couch, but no amount of adjusting could make me comfortable. I finally gave up asking my kids to move the pillows around and tried to just ignore the pain. I wanted to sleep peacefully, but even that was proving to be too big a challenge. I didn't even consider going downstairs that day. It wasn't worth it.

As the sun went down, I began dreading the long night ahead. Hours upon hours with no distractions, no interruptions, nothing to take my mind off of my situation. Just me, my pain, and my thoughts.

McCall helped me get ready for bed and situated me on the couch in a position that was the least painful. The couch, which had at first seemed like a sanctuary from the torture of my bed, had turned against me, too. There wasn't anywhere I could escape. Even my dreams, which used to take me to the beautiful place, were no longer safe. What was I supposed to do?

I only slept for a short time before the crawly things from the shadows chased me back into waking. My body ached, and I could tell my back was going to be stiff the next morning. I wanted to move to get more comfortable, but I couldn't do it by myself. And since no position actually relieved the pain, what would be the point of waking someone else up to help me?

I lay there feeling helpless and hopeless. Tears began to roll down my cheeks. I didn't want to do this. I couldn't endure it any longer. I'd thought I'd be fine once I got out of the hospital. I was wrong. I'd thought I'd feel more comfortable in my own bed. I was wrong. I'd thought I could go back to doing simple things, like climbing the stairs, washing my own hair, or even just sleeping. I was wrong. I was wrong about all of it.

Was this going to be what it was like from now on? Was I going to need help to accomplish every little task? Was I going to have to be looked after constantly, like an aging parent in a nursing home? Would every moment be filled with pain, and my greatest accomplishments consist of walking to the bathroom by myself and drinking chicken broth?

If that was life, maybe it would have been better if I hadn't survived.

My eyes wandered to the window, which was closed to keep out the winter chill. I thought about ending the pain, just falling, falling, falling, until I hit the ground and didn't have to suffer anymore. No more pain, no more enduring the stairs, the bed, and the couch, no more feelings of uselessness. I could return to the beautiful place and just stay there forever. All with one little jump.

Of course, to do that, I'd have to actually climb out the window. In my current state, that was next to impossible.

Lucky me. I was in too much pain to even have the option of ending the pain.

I looked away from the window toward the bed, where McCall was sleeping. Even as I entertained thoughts of dying, I knew I couldn't. I had three kids, and they needed me to be strong. They needed me to fight my way through this.

They hadn't given up. I couldn't give up either.

They were the thing I could hold onto.

I wish I could say that I fell asleep right then and was finally able to rest, but that wouldn't be true. The rest of the night was still torture. I still suffered through the nightmares and woke up in the dark, longing for morning to come. I still wondered if it would have been better if I hadn't survived the surgeries. I still wrestled with despair and thought about quitting. My sense of worthlessness still warred with my stubbornness and my love for my kids.

The truth is, every night was like that for a long time. You can't conquer this kind of problem with a single battle. I had many more battles ahead of me.

But at least I'd won this one.

11
PERSEVERANCE

Sunday, November 4

A few hours into the night, I realized I needed to use the bathroom. I looked around, not wanting to wake McCall up. *Okay*, I thought, *you can do this. It's just walking to the bathroom. You did it in the hospital. Piece of cake.*

I moved a few pillows aside, and while my chest hurt with every movement, I stayed quiet. All I needed to do was stand up, and then I knew I could shamble into the bathroom on my own. I leaned over and placed my hands on my knees. One, two, three, go.

I used my legs to rock my body forward into a standing position, and I cried out in pain.

McCall jumped out of bed. "Mom, what are you doing?"

I wavered on unsteady feet, trying to find my balance. "I need to go to the bathroom. I didn't want to wake you up."

"Are you crazy? That's why I'm here, to help you." She hurried over and took my arm to help me balance.

I immediately felt embarrassed by my near-fall. "Sorry, girl," I said. "I just thought I could do it by myself."

"Not yet," she said as she helped me to the bathroom.

Afterward, she made me as comfortable as possible back on the couch. The rest of the night crawled by, but after one of my fitful sleeps I woke to see light. Finally it was morning.

McCall must have developed a sixth sense about when I was awake, because she rose a few minutes later. "Good morning."

"Morning," I said. I wasn't sure yet if it was good. "Sorry I had such a restless night."

"I just wish there was something I could do."

I sighed. "There's nothing anyone can do. But I'm sure things will get better soon. I think one of the meds I'm taking is too strong, and that's why I'm so jumpy and irritated. I might need something different."

"For sure," McCall said. "I'll call the doctor's office and see if they can prescribe something else."

Hopefully that would put an end to those creepy-crawly dreams.

After a light breakfast and my morning medication, McCall helped me undress for a shower. "Oh, we need to weigh you," she commented.

"We do? Why?"

"Dr. Schorlemmer and the nurses want me to track your weight and take your blood pressure at least three times each day."

I groaned. "Really? Okay, fine."

She helped me step on the scale. The number read 163.

No way. I'd been home for a couple days, eating hardly anything and using the bathroom all the time. How could I still have over thirty pounds left to lose? I glanced at myself in the mirror and quickly looked away.

McCall noticed. "Mom, it's okay. It's just water weight, remember?"

I wanted to cry. I knew the water weight was a minor issue. I really did. But I had worked so hard to get into shape before all of this happened. To have that snatched away so suddenly was heartbreaking. I was terrified that I would look this way forever. And if this minor problem took so long to solve, what did it mean for the bigger problems?

I pushed all thought of that out of my mind. I didn't understand it, and I didn't want to think about it. The less I worried myself, the better.

After I showered, the day's visitors began to arrive. I phased in and out of coherence, drifting off to sleep only to be startled back into waking. McCall kept control of everything, making sure I took my meds, ate and drank, and had my blood pressure checked regularly. Some friends brought dinner over and came up to see me. Like everyone else, they had that familiar look of love in their eyes. It encouraged me to know that my friends supported us so much.

I wanted to try the dinner that they brought, if only because of how overwhelmed I felt by the outpouring of love. And I wanted to eat like a regular person, which meant I needed to go downstairs to the kitchen. I knew it would be hard, but I'd spent the entire day in my room. I needed a change.

With my kids holding me up, the trip down wasn't too bad. It felt wonderful to sit down at the kitchen table and eat dinner with my family. My kids all seemed happy that I was there, and while I didn't eat much, I stayed with them as long as I could. However, I soon realized I needed to go back upstairs.

Those stairs. Those awful, horrible, torturous stairs. I had run up them a zillion times without even thinking twice, and now they were the bane of my existence. I hated them, just like I hated the bed and the couch. Which one I hated the most depended on what I was doing at the time, but while climbing, it was definitely the stairs.

The boys helped me up, step by agonizing step. I shook as they brought me over to the couch and settled me in. The TV was on, so I flipped through the channels a bit. The news covered the aftermath of Hurricane Sandy on the east coast. I watched interviews with people who had lost everything, and I felt for them. I was also amazed by the number of volunteers who came out to help in that time of devastation. It made me even more grateful for all of the people who rallied around our family. I was truly blessed to have such an amazing support team.

McCall brought me my nighttime meds. "You have a new pain med," she said. "Dr. Schorlemmer called in a lighter dose, so hopefully no more hallucinating or agitation during the night. Do you want to change clothes?"

I shook my head, just wanting to take the lighter medication and fall asleep for some real rest. "No, I'm too tired." I didn't even have the energy to brush my teeth. I wanted to curl up in a ball in my bed, but instead I was stuck on this uncomfortable couch. My back was already protesting, but there wasn't anything to be done.

I drifted off.

I woke again shortly after.

Fortunately I wasn't seeing the crawly things and I didn't feel jumpy. I was just awake. And miserable. And uncomfortable. This night dragged on like the previous one, with the same struggles and the same emotional roller coaster.

But like the previous night, morning came.

My restlessness had kept McCall up most of the night, so I didn't want to wake her again when I realized I needed to use the bathroom. It hadn't gone well the day before, but I thought I'd try it by myself again. I adjusted my position, moving slowly, my body stiff and sore from the long night. I made it to a standing position, which brought on a whole new set of pains, as well as dizziness and a pounding in my chest. I paused to regroup and glanced toward the bed. McCall was still asleep. Good. I could do this.

I slowly started toward the bathroom, and finally made it to the toilet. I was out of breath, but I did it. Score one for Team Teri!

After McCall awoke and we went through the rest of my morning routine—a small breakfast, meds, a shower, weighing in, still feeling fat, getting dressed, fixing hair, brushing teeth, and finally settling back down on the couch—Ruth the home healthcare nurse came by to check on me. She removed some of the medical strips from my chest and groin area, and told me everything was healing fine. No infection. And on Friday, my home healthcare physical therapist would come to start working with me.

Finally, I thought. Physical therapy would be the path back to normality.

I couldn't wait to get started.

Another night, another battle, another victory of willpower. Another sunrise to mark the end of the night. Step by step, I kept going, just like when climbing the stairs.

In the morning I noticed that McCall had left my phone on the ottoman. I realized I probably had a ton of messages, so I thought I should start looking through them. I picked up the phone and began looking through the texts from the past several days.

I read the first few and started to cry. Not from pain this time, but from gratitude. There were so many messages, each expressing their love and concern and offering their support and prayer. My friends. My family. Such an amazing support team. "You're an amazing woman, and you're going to make it through this." "Just wanted to say how much we love you and your kids." "I can't believe this. Sending many prayers your way." These were all for me.

After reading the texts I discovered a ton of voicemail messages as well, but I was too overwhelmed to even listen to them. Tears poured down my cheeks and dripped on the phone, and I couldn't stop myself from sobbing out loud.

McCall woke up and saw me crying. "Mom, what's wrong? Why are you crying?"

I showed her the texts. "You're all doing so much for me. All the messages and the flowers and the support. It's so much. I'm so sorry for this whole thing."

McCall began to cry too. "Mom, please don't get down. You're doing so good and making such great progress. We all *want* to help you. All these people came by the hospital while you were there, and some didn't even get a chance to see you. This is our way of giving back to you for everything you've given us."

"But it's just so much. And I don't know how long this is going to last. And I don't know why this had to happen to me." The tears of gratitude began to mix with tears of frustration. "It's just so hard!"

"I know, Mom. I know."

We both cried some more.

McCall hugged me and wiped her eyes. "Don't feel stressed about people trying to help. We just want you to get better."

"I will," I murmured. "I promise." I dried my tears and tried to smile. "Sorry to be so emotional today."

"It's okay," she said. "How about this: no visitors today. Just rest. We'll watch a movie or something."

"That would be nice."

"And the boys will be here for dinner."

I brightened at that news. I loved it when all three of my kids were together with me. It reminded me of why I continued to fight through this.

I slept through most of the day, and when dinner time came I didn't feel like tackling the stairs, so the kids brought a plate up and sat with me while I ate.

While we were all together, we shared a family prayer. It was important to us to pray together, but as the kids had grown up and moved away, the tradition had sort of fallen into disuse. It felt good to revitalize it. Dallin offered the prayer that night. I sat on the couch, and my kids all kneeled around me. We bowed our heads in reverence, and Dallin began.

"Thank you, Heavenly Father, for the miracle of our mom's life. Thank you for the love and support we've been given during this difficult time. Our hearts are so full from all your many blessings. Please give her continued strength through this recovery journey, and help us to be strong for her. Me and my brother and sister need her, and we are so grateful that we didn't lose her."

He poured his heart out for several minutes before concluding, "Amen." We were all in tears by the time he finished. I thanked my kids for being so wonderful. They thanked me for hanging on. We settled down to sleep, and I faced up with another long night and another battle.

12
THE SMALL STUFF

Wednesday, November 7 – Thursday, November 8

After being home for most of a week, every night was still the same. Pain in my back. Pain in my tailbone. Pain in my chest. Leaning forward, hunching over a lap pillow they'd given me at the hospital to relieve the pressure and give my back a break. Falling asleep, only to wake up and despair over the fact that it was still dark. Checking the time on my phone. One thirty. Two thirty. Three thirty. Wanting sleep, but every part of my body hurting. Every. Single. Part.

Finally waking to see light outside.

Feeling overwhelming gratitude that it was morning.

I made it to the bathroom and back without waking McCall up—another minor victory to celebrate. I found the TV remote and flipped through a few channels until I found The Today Show. It had been over ten years since I'd really watched it, but for want of distraction, I stopped to see what they were discussing. I recognized some of the faces—Matt Lauer and Al—but there were several new people too—Savannah, Natalie, Willie, Tamryn. There were some serious news stories, but they also did a lot of kooky things. I watched their antics, chuckling and feeling completely entertained, my mind taken away from my misery for a while. Their personalities formed a fun combination, and it made me happy to watch them.

An hour flew by before McCall woke up. "Hey," she said. "How long have you been awake?"

"Like an hour or so. The Today Show is so funny!" I said.

She rolled out of bed. "I'll get you some breakfast. Do you need to use the bathroom?"

"Oh, no, I already went."

"Mom!" She gave me a disapproving look. "You need to wake me up so I can help you with that."

"I can do it by myself."

"But what if..."

I started to feel defensive of my ever-so-small victories. "McCall, it's the only thing I can do on my own anymore. Please, just let me do it." I remembered how worried she and the boys had been over these past weeks, and I tried to reassure her. "I'm fine, I promise."

She flashed another disapproving look, but gave in. "Okay. But if you do need help, please let me know."

"I will, girl. Thanks."

She went downstairs and came back a few minutes later with yogurt, a banana, and some toast. Since I'd showered the night before, she just helped me to change and weighed me.

Still 163. Boo. Would this water weight go away already?

After getting ready for the day, Ruth stopped by to check my vitals. My blood pressure was up a little higher than it should have been, so she called Dr. Schorlemmer to check with him. He said since I would be seeing him on Tuesday, he'd change a few of my meds then.

Then it came time for her to check on my incisions. I looked at the walls, the ceiling, the hallway—anything to avoid having to see my Halloween-costume body. She removed a bunch more of the medical strips and uncovered part of the incision on my chest. I winced, not from pain, but from the thought of my appearance. It had to be awful—row upon row of stitches running down my torso.

To my surprise, she said, "Wow, that's looking really good."

Seriously? In spite of my determination not to, I looked down.

She was right. I was amazed at how well the surgical incisions had healed. Instead of stitches, I saw a thin line. It was red, but that would fade. It didn't look like a zipper at all.

"You'll still need to keep all the areas clean and dry," she said, "but we'll probably have all the strips off by next week. Now, how are you getting up and around?"

"Er, okay," I said. "It's hard, but I can make it to the bathroom on my own now."

"Excellent. Are you eating much?"

"Just a little. I get full too fast."

"That's okay. How about pain? Are you able to manage it okay?"

"I'm fine." I hesitated. That wasn't completely true. "Except for nights. Sleeping is nearly impossible. I really wish I could lie down in my bed."

The nurse nodded sympathetically. "I know. You'll be able to do it eventually, I promise. But it could be several more weeks before your chest can handle the pressure of lying down. It's a common thing after such extensive open heart surgery."

I didn't say anything, but my thoughts went nuts. *What? Several more weeks?* She had to be joking, right? How was I supposed to handle weeks more of sleeping on that evil couch?

I calmed myself down before I could start to worry. *It will all be okay*, I thought. *It will all be okay.* I was exhausted and frustrated when the nurse eventually left, so I went straight to sleep.

It was afternoon when I woke up. McCall was in the room, keeping an eye on me. "Wow," she said. "You slept for a long time. Do you remember what you were dreaming about? You kept talking in your sleep."

"No." I smiled. It had felt good to get some real rest. "What was I saying?"

"A lot of things that didn't make sense. It was funny. A few times I thought you were awake. Here, I'll bring you up some lunch."

Despite having slept for hours, my body felt awful—so stiff and sore. "I think it might be good for me to go downstairs to eat," I said. I would tackle the stairs in exchange for giving some relief to my aching back.

We made it down the stairs without too much trouble, and I was able to eat a little lunch at the kitchen table. My mouth and throat felt a little better than they had in the days prior, but still nothing tasted right except soda, and even that burned going down. I wished food would taste normal again. My mouth hadn't even been part of the surgery, so why was it fighting with me, too?

After lunch McCall helped me back up the stairs, step by agonizing step. My legs turned to jelly, and I had to bend over to relieve some of the pain when we reached the top, but McCall seemed relieved that we made it at all. "Good job, Mom!" she said.

She settled me on my couch and gave me some more meds, which helped me to doze off despite the discomfort. I felt that familiar sense of floating, drifting through the air as sights, sounds, and places rushed by me. None of them stayed long, and I could barely even make them out. My head swirled with thoughts and visions. Nothing made sense. Where was I? Where was I meant to be? How could I get there? Where was the beautiful place?

I actually woke up to hear myself talking. I had no idea what I was saying, but I definitely sleep-talked myself into waking. I glanced over at McCall, who saw that I was awake and stopped stifling the laughter she was holding in. The situation was so funny that I started laughing too. "What was I even saying?" I laughed.

"I have *no* idea," she said.

Despite that moment of humor, I didn't feel very well throughout the rest of the evening. I had little energy as my visitors stopped by, and by the time night came I could barely get ready for bed. I stayed awake watching TV as long as I could, reasoning that if I was exhausted enough, I'd sleep better.

It didn't work. The night was again pure misery.

But I got to watch The Today Show again in the morning, which was some consolation. They mentioned that it was now Thursday, November 8. How did that happen? Where had the time gone?

My friends Wendy, Devi, and Laurel came over with sandwiches that afternoon. We visited for a while, and I talked about some things I remembered about the night I went to the ER. They told me how they'd come to see me when I was in the hospital, and how hard it was to see me like that. Of course I didn't remember those times, but the conversation reminded me again of how wonderful and amazing my friends are. I didn't know what my kids or I would have done without them. You never know how many supporters you have until disaster strikes and they all come through. It was truly humbling and inspiring.

My friend Klistia brought dinner over. She didn't stay long, since she could see that I was tired, but we did talk for a little while. She told me I was her hero.

She, and all the others who rallied around me, were mine.

After Klistia left, McCall helped me downstairs for some dinner. I ate only a little, and I noticed that the kitchen counter was again full of goodies that people had brought by. I spotted a plate of brownies, which looked delicious. My taste buds hadn't been working properly since the surgery, but for some reason I really had a craving for a brownie. This was weird, because I had never liked chocolate before.

"Hey, McCall, can you bring me one of those chocolate things?" I asked.

She gave me a strange look. "What?"

"I want to try one. They look delicious."

"Really?" She seemed dubious. "You really want something chocolate?"

"Yeah. For some reason it sounds good. I just want to try it."

McCall shrugged and brought the brownie over. It smelled wonderful, and I took a bite, expecting it to taste strange, like everything else.

Holy cow. It was amazing. I devoured the whole thing.

McCall was shocked. "I can't believe you ate that. That's crazy."

"I know, right?" I said. I thought about eating another one, just because it tasted so good, but my stomach was full, and it was getting late. I still had those stairs ahead of me, too.

Once again we climbed the mountain, one heartbreaking step at a time. It was all I could do to lift my legs up the last few steps. As usual I was at my breaking point.

How could it be so hard just to walk up the stairs? Or sleep in a bed? Or eat normal food? It just didn't make sense.

Another awful night, battling the pain in my body and the demons in my thoughts. Another blessed sunrise after it.

I woke up to see Jace in my bed, sound asleep. He must have come in sometime during the night. I watched The Today Show quietly, not wanting to wake him or McCall. I again stood up and walked to the bathroom by myself, pushing through the shakiness and dizziness. I needed to do this by myself, if only to feel like I was making progress. It was the one thing I could handle, and I held onto that with every last ounce of strength.

The kids woke up shortly after I made it back to the couch and told me I was talking crazy throughout the night. I knew it. My dreams flew from place to place like a roller coaster ride. We laughed about my sleep talking. At least it meant I was sleeping.

When McCall took my blood pressure, it was even higher than the day before. I didn't feel very well, either. My home physical therapist was supposed to come by that afternoon, but when he called to confirm I reluctantly told him my symptoms. I wanted to push through everything, but it wouldn't help if I made it worse by trying too hard on a bad day. The physical therapist decided I should see Dr. Schorlemmer and get my blood pressure regulated before we started sessions.

As we hung up, I actually felt relief, not disappointment. I knew I wasn't up to it today. Sometimes, hard as it was, I had to admit when I needed to slow down.

I hoped when I saw the doctor next week, he'd have some good news to cheer me up and encourage me.

***

Tuesday, November 13

Ten days after leaving the hospital, I went back to see Dr. Schorlemmer. McCall drove, and I rode in silence, trying to anticipate every bump or vibration of the car. All movement made my chest tighten with pain. When our car came anywhere close to the car in front of us, I tensed up and braced myself as terror kicked in. If the airbag went off, I knew it would kill me. McCall drove cautiously, but I still felt freaked out.

I was a mess by the time we reached the hospital. We pulled up, and McCall hopped out. "I'll grab you a wheelchair."

Despite being in tremendous pain, I objected, "I don't need a wheelchair."

She wisely ignored me and brought one out anyway. She and the valet helped me out of the car and into the wheelchair. I was shaking, freezing, and feeling like I wanted to scream. I doubted my legs would have supported me for two steps. I reluctantly admitted that McCall was right, and looked up at her. "Thanks."

"Of course." She noticed me getting teary. "Mom, don't cry. It's okay. You just think you can do more than you really can. It's how you always are. It's okay."

We arrived at the office, and a nurse escorted us back to the exam rooms. She weighed me, took my vitals, and commented on how well I was doing. *Uh-huh*, I wanted to reply. *Just tell me when I'll be back to normal.*

Dr. Schorlemmer walked in with his signature huge smile, and as usual, I couldn't help but smile back. Regardless of how I was doing, he'd saved my life. I would be forever grateful to him.

"How's my miracle girl doing?" he asked.

"I'm good."

"You look good." He sat down in front of me. "How are you feeling?"

Time to be honest. "I guess I'm okay, under the circumstances. I don't have any energy, though. And this extra weight I'm carrying around makes it even worse. It's not coming off."

He looked at my chart. "Yes, you do have a little extra water weight."

I blinked. "A little? Look at me. It's over thirty pounds."

"Well, your kidneys are fully functional now. I can give you a prescription to help you shed the water weight, though you'll be up using the bathroom a lot. Are you up to it?"

"Yes," I answered immediately. "I'll live in the bathroom if I have to."

He laughed. "Okay. Make sure you record your weight every morning."

"We do. Thank you so much." There was one point of encouragement. I hoped for a few more.

He made some notes and then changed the topic. "How are you sleeping?"

"Awful." I wanted to be honest with the doctor, especially since he had kept me alive. "I can't lay down in my bed, so I'm sleeping propped up on a couch in my room. It's horrible."

"That's not unexpected," he said. "Your chest is still healing. It's not ready for the pressure of lying down yet."

"How much longer will it be?" I asked. I held my breath as I waited for the answer.

It wasn't what I wanted. "It could be another four weeks or so," he said. "It varies from patient to patient. Just keep trying to lie down from time to time. Eventually you'll be able to do it."

My heart sank. Four more weeks of sleeping on that awful couch? How was I going to handle that?

At the same time, though, I felt a bit relieved. At least what I was experiencing was normal. There was an end in sight. I just had to stick it out until then.

We went over my appetite and the rawness in my throat, which he said was from the ventilator and should go away in a week or so. He made a few adjustments in my medications and explained a few more details about my recovery. "You're doing amazingly well," he said. "Your home healthcare nurses will keep me posted on your progress and your vitals, so I'll see you again in four weeks."

"Hopefully by then I'll be sleeping in my bed," I said.

He chuckled. "Hopefully. You're doing great, Teri."

Tears filled my eyes as I looked at him. "Thank you for saving my life," I whispered, wrapping him in a hug.

He hugged me gently in return. "It wasn't just me. I'm just grateful that you're still with us." As we broke the hug, he smiled at me. "Just hang in there. You're on your way back. You'll get there soon."

Seeing the doctor again encouraged me and helped my determination to heal.

Riding home in the car and climbing the stairs sent me spiraling into despair again. Life had become a zigzagging wave of highs and lows—gratitude and joy broken by pain and frustration. The former got me through the latter, but I didn't know how long I could keep it up.

If only soon was now.

13
PHYSICAL THERAPY

My home physical therapist, Dan, came later that day, bringing some equipment in a large bag. We went over the basics of my medical state, and then he explained that we were going to start my "rehabilitation."

Really? Rehabilitation? That was what you needed to do after you broke your limbs in a car accident or had a nasty fall. I didn't need rehab; I was progressing just fine. Dr. Schorlemmer had said himself that I should be able to sleep in my own bed in a few weeks. It couldn't take long after that for me to be back to my routine.

Bottom line: This would be no big deal.

He set up a folding chair in my room about fifteen feet from my bedroom door and had me sit down in it. *Great,* I thought. *Sitting is easy.* I'd been practicing sitting twenty-four seven since I got out of the hospital.

"Now," he said, "I want you to stand up, walk to the bedroom door, and then come back and sit down. I'm going to time you."

"Okay," I said, trying not to think of this as a race. Obviously I'd be slower than normal, but how hard could this be?

"Ready...go."

I stood up and steadied myself. I started walking toward the door, confident that I could complete this distance on my own. While climbing the stairs or lying down were still out, I had been doing okay with walking.

The door seemed to be approaching very, very slowly, and I wondered how much time had elapsed. This was taking longer than I expected. It was only fifteen feet, though, so maybe that was just my imagination.

I made it to the door and started back. Again, the walk seemed to take longer than expected. I felt a little freaked out. Was time moving too fast, or was I really moving as slowly as it seemed?

I finally reached the chair and sat back down. The therapist nodded. "Good job."

I noticed he hadn't said my time. "How long did I take?" I asked.

"Thirty-nine seconds."

Holy crap. What? Just to get up and walk to the door and back? That would take maybe ten seconds if I was healthy. I hadn't thought it could possibly take more than twenty—twenty-five tops now.

So much for this being simple. Ugh.

Next Dan pulled out a small, portable pedal bike thing and put it on the ground in front of the chair. I put my feet on the pedals, remembering how I used to ride my bike outdoors. I had never really enjoyed stationary bikes, though I rode them on occasion at the gym. This was just like that, except I was sitting in a regular chair. I started to pedal around and around, and it actually seemed pretty easy.

"Good," he said. "I want you to do this for ten minutes. Do you think you can?"

"Of course," I said. "No problem." Finally, something resembling real exercise.

A couple minutes in, I realized I might have overestimated my stamina. Tiredness set in, and it took more and more effort to keep the pedals going around.

After five minutes, Dan noticed that I was weary. "Are you okay?" he asked.

"Yup, I'm doing great." I tried not to let my face betray the lie. My legs became heavier and heavier, and I started to sweat, but I doggedly kept pedaling. I couldn't give up, not on something this simple. My aching chest started to throb, and I wanted to scream. Why was this stupid little thing so difficult? Irrationally, I started to blame the pedals, the walking, the chair, the therapist—anything to explain away why I wasn't able to make this work. I knew, though, that the problem wasn't with any of them. It was with me.

By the time the ten minutes were up, I felt both frustrated and furious, though I tried not to let it show.

"How do you feel?" asked the therapist.

"Fine," I said. I knew he had to have picked up on some of my anger, so I admitted, "It was a little harder than I thought it would be."

"Well, it's only your first day. You're doing awesome, considering that. We'll see what happens next time."

Yes, next time, I thought. *Next time I'll beat you, you stupid little pedal thing.*

I thought we were done, but he asked if I could do one more set of exercises. I immediately said yes, though my body cried no.

I slowly stood up, and he had me put my hands on my dresser to keep my balance. Then he had me do front leg lifts, side leg lifts, and back leg lifts, ten reps each. Simple, ridiculous exercises that horrified me by how difficult they were. It took all of my strength to complete the repetitions. I was glad I could hold onto the dresser. If it wasn't there, I would have fallen, and I didn't think I'd be able to get up again.

"Great work," he said. For a second I thought he was going to tell me to do another set, and I mentally begged the universe for anything but that. "I think that's all we'll do for now."

Thank goodness.

He pulled out a sheet of paper with instructions on exercises he wanted me to do each day. I promised to follow them, but I just wanted him to leave. I was done. I was so done.

He gathered up his supplies and said he'd see me on Friday.

"Sounds good, see you then," I said.

He left.

I started to cry.

I put the instructions on the dresser, not sure I would follow them. I didn't want to do this anymore. Why was everything so hard? Why was I so weak? Why couldn't I do even the simplest task without it being a huge undertaking?

As the next week passed, one good thing happened. I began to shed the water weight. Each morning, one or two pounds would drop off the scale, which pleased me to no end. I didn't even mind all the extra trips to the bathroom. Maybe that would help me move faster next time I had to walk to the bedroom door and back.

Visitors flowed through the house, overwhelming me with their love and support. And food. Lots of food. I was still in enormous pain, and the nights were still awful. I dreamt of being near the beautiful place—a place with no pain. I wanted to find a way inside and stay there, but I had to wake up to reality—a reality where I saw little progress in my ongoing physical therapy sessions and no improvement in my ability to climb the blasted stairs, which continued to kick my butt every time. I tried and failed again to get comfortable lying in bed. The PT exercises, which I eventually relented and began doing, remained strenuous. Every time I slept, I wished I could grab the beautiful place and drag it with me into my waking life. It came to represent my end goal—a return to normality. All I wanted to do was reach it.

Four weeks after my surgeries, my family decided to have Thanksgiving at my brother's house, ten minutes away, instead of my mom's house, which was two hours away. A two-hour drive should have been no big deal, but I dreaded even the ten minutes spent in the car.

Why was this aortic dissection thing so freaking hard to recover from? I grabbed my iPad and decided to Google it. Enough of not knowing. It was time to figure out exactly what I was fighting. When the search came up, I clicked on a website that looked informative.

The first statistic I read said that the mortality rate for aortic dissections was eighty percent. Of those eighty percent, fifty percent died before ever getting to the hospital. Of the twenty percent who actually survived the surgery, thirty percent died after surgery. I felt my hands start to shake. This was scary.

I tried to make sense of the words describing a dissection, but it was like another language. The terms and phrases on the screen overwhelmed me, and I changed my mind. I didn't want to read about this. I didn't want to know.

I deleted the search.

I couldn't face it yet. I needed to keep my hopes up. I needed to keep pushing forward. I needed to reach the beautiful place. I knew that with just a little more time, I could get there. I realized again that I might be in denial, but I was okay with that. If I could deny this thing out of its power over my life, I'd deny it all the way.

14
GIVING THANKS

Thursday, November 22

Thanksgiving arrived cold, with scattered snow over the preceding few days. I had dropped about fifteen pounds, though I still had about twenty more to go. None of my regular clothes fit. McCall helped me dress in sweats and pull my hair up in a ponytail. It wasn't holiday attire at all, but I was still excited to go.

Jace and McCall helped me out to the car. The car ride was uncomfortable, but at least it was only ten minutes long. Changing the location of the dinner had been a good idea. I trembled with a chill as we walked to the house, our feet crunching in the light dusting of snow.

Warmth greeted us as we entered. "Aunt Teri is here!" someone yelled. My mom came to give me a hug, tears in her eyes. Dallin, who had driven there from his home, embraced all of us. My brother, sister-in-law, nieces, and nephews were all there, and I began to get choked up. My recovery was hard, but it was worth it, because I could still be here with all of them. My little brother and his family weren't able to make the trip from California, since they had traveled to be here for me less than a month ago after the surgery, but they were with us in spirit.

McCall made me comfortable in a cozy chair by the fire while everyone helped with the finishing touches for dinner. We visited and laughed about old times, remembered Thanksgivings past, and speculated about what all of the cousins were doing. At dinner we sat around the table and took turns saying what we were thankful for. My newly-married niece and her husband both expressed thanks for all the love and support and work that went into making their wedding day special. Multiple people were thankful for work and for the opportunity of education. Of course everyone mentioned my amazing survival. We talked about our gratitude for the army of friends that came and surrounded us with love and support, and continued to do so even now. We all became very emotional as we expressed our love for one another and our gratitude to our father in heaven for blessing our lives.

The food smelled wonderful as it was passed around the table. Hot turkey and stuffing, creamy mashed potatoes and gravy, sweet potatoes, crispy salad, Grandma's homemade cranberry sauce, homemade rolls—so much yummy food. I was actually hungry—yet another thing for which to be thankful. We ate, talked, and enjoyed one another's company. I became full pretty quickly, which was disappointing since everything was so delicious, but no one seemed to mind.

After dinner, McCall helped me back to the chair by the fire and covered me with a blanket. I dozed off for a while, but woke in time for dessert.

Grandma had made fresh homemade pies, something we looked forward to every year. I managed to eat a bite of banana cream, which was everyone's favorite. She'd also baked a rich pumpkin pie and a beautiful, golden-crusted apple pie. Almost everyone tried a piece of each kind. So delicious.

As the festivities wound down, everyone moved to different rooms to either nap or watch sports. I'd lasted about four hours, and the evening sky had begun fading to dark, so my kids and I said our goodbyes and headed home. Grandma made sure we took plenty of leftovers with us.

At home, the boys helped me climb the stairs, and then McCall and I watched TV together while they went back downstairs to watch football.

I needed to bathe before bed, so after McCall helped me into the shower, I leaned forward to let the warm water soothe my aching back. I discovered I could bend further now, so I checked on the incisions on my right leg. They all seemed to be healing nicely—another blessing.

I noticed that my legs were extremely hairy—I'd never seen them so grown out before. I could feel it under my arms, too. I looked at my razor on the shower rack and contemplated shaving, but I didn't think I could do it today. I was already out of energy, plus I was a bit shaky. No sense in risking more incisions when the ones I already had were almost healed. Maybe I could do it tomorrow.

McCall helped me dry off after the shower, and I was pleased to see that the weight loss was showing and the scars on my chest were healing nicely. They looked a lot less scary, though I still didn't like to see myself this way.

McCall spent the rest of Thanksgiving weekend decorating the house for Christmas. I watched, gave advice, and helped a little with decorating the trees. *For sure*, I thought, *I'll be better by Christmas*. I just had to keep fighting a little while longer.

In the last week of November, my physical therapist stopped by again, and we went through my little workout routine. The following week, I would start real cardiac rehab. I was pleased to discover that the pedal bike workout wasn't as taxing this week, and I could do the standing exercises with less difficulty, too—more and more reasons for gratitude. It truly was the season of thanks. Even the stairs were becoming less of a pain—they were still difficult, and I still needed help, but I could maintain my composure when I reached the top.

It had been five weeks. The recovery was taking its time. I needed to go back to work soon and get back to my normal life. It was encouraging to see those bits of progress.

Even the smallest victories counted. Since I'd missed my hair appointment at the end of October, the silvery gray had grown out a lot. One night my hairdresser, Larissa, made a house call. As I sat in a chair in the kitchen, she gave me a touch-up bleach job to hide the gray until I was strong enough to come in for a real hair appointment. The next day, I wore my hair down for the first time since my surgeries. Another minor victory, another step toward wholeness. At this rate, I was certain that everything would return to normal in December.

15
PARTIES AND PRAYERS

Tuesday, December 4 – Friday, December 7

After a particularly long and miserable night, The Today Show informed me that it was Tuesday, December 4.

The day before my daughter's twentieth birthday.

What was I going to do for her? I couldn't buy her a gift; I couldn't drive to go shopping. How could I surprise her without any mobility?

I looked over at her, asleep in my bed. She had barely left my side for six weeks. She'd helped with every single need that came up. I couldn't have survived without her. I was sure she'd rather be out with friends, finishing up her fall semester at school and doing normal college student things, but instead she'd put her life on hold to take care of me. Of course my boys were there for me too, but there was something different about my youngest child, my unexpected miracle baby, my only daughter being there in this way. I can't explain it, but there's a unique bond between a mother and a daughter, and I felt like this ordeal had tested that bond and forged it into something unbreakable. My baby girl had grown up into a beautiful, amazing woman, and I admired her strength and maturity at such a young age.

I had to think of a way to make her birthday special. I would need help. But I'd already imposed on everyone so much. Who was I going to ask to pitch in on this?

It turned out I needn't have worried.

Later that day, my friend Julie called to tell me she and her daughters were going to bring sandwiches over the following night to have a little party for McCall. Another friend, Lindsi, said she'd picked up some things for McCall's birthday. A third friend, Val, stopped by with a bag full of clothes from Macy's and a red velvet Bundt cake, and yet another friend, Laura, came by after work with some gifts, another cake, and balloons.

Once again, my friends came through for my family. I could not be more blessed. I was overjoyed that we would be able to celebrate McCall's birthday and give her a well-deserved party.

We had just a small get-together—me, McCall, Dallin, Jace, Julie and her two daughters, and another friend of McCall's. She opened her gifts, we sang happy birthday, and we ate cake. That was a full night for me, so we were done by about seven p.m. McCall and the other girls left after that for a birthday party that another friend was throwing for her, and I went to sleep.

The next day, December 6, was the day of my first cardiac rehab appointment. I felt bad that McCall had to spend so much of her birthday week driving me to and from the hospital, but I felt a little better knowing that we'd celebrated on the actual day.

It had been a little over six weeks since the surgeries, and two weeks since I'd last been in the car. I dreaded buckling myself into the seat, but it turned out that the ride wasn't that bad. As we pulled up to the valet parking, I looked at McCall and grinned. "No wheelchair this time. I can walk."

She laughed. "Okay, Mom."

We took the elevator to the third floor and walked around the corner to the cardiac rehab unit. McCall took my coat and went to hang out in a small waiting area.

I took a deep breath and walked up to the desk. Another day, another challenge to meet.

The lady at the desk recognized me. "So you're the one everyone has been talking about around here," she said. "You're famous. Do you know that you're a miracle?"

I laughed. "Yes, I've heard that a few times."

"We're so glad you're still with us. My name's Leslee. I'll help you get started here."

She showed me where to pick up my portable heart monitor and check in with the attending therapist, who was sitting behind the counter with several computer screens. Leslee explained that they would log me in and monitor my heart activity on the screens during the rehab session. Then she took me to yet another area and brought out these four sticky pads that she applied to my skin, under my shirt. The portable heart monitor had four cords that snapped onto the four sticky things. Leslee said that I could hook up the equipment myself in the future, but I must have looked confused. She smiled. "Don't worry. We're always here to help you, and there are directions posted right here." She then put my monitor in a container that hung around my neck and proclaimed me ready to go.

We went over to a recumbent stationary bike, and she helped me sit down on it. I remembered the difficulty I'd had with the little pedal bike at my home, and I worried that she was going to ask too much of me.

"We're going to see if you can go for seven minutes," she said.

Only seven? "What resistance level should I put it on?" I asked, sure that there must be a catch.

Leslee smiled. "No resistance today."

Only seven minutes with no resistance? Easy. I had this in the bag.

I began cycling with great energy, happy that I was able to exercise— sort of—once more. After a couple of minutes, I started to feel the burn in my legs and chest. My enthusiasm waned. This was much harder than I expected. How could it still be so difficult after all the work I'd put into my recovery?

It took all I had to finish the seven minutes. Leslee came over to take my blood pressure and check my oxygen levels. My results must have been good, because her face lit up. "You did great."

I didn't respond. I was too disappointed in myself. Maybe I could make it up in the next exercise.

She led me over to the treadmills. "We'll try this now for seven minutes." She set the speed to one point five miles per hour and gave me an apologetic look. "I know it's slow, but we need to see how you do."

I was tired after the bike, but I still found it ridiculous that I had to walk at such a slow speed. I began walking at my one point five miles per hour, feeling silly, but trying to keep a positive mindset. At least I could be sure I would finish this.

Then I glanced to the left. Beside me walked an older gentleman, probably eighty years old. His back hunched over and he had an oxygen tube in his nose.

Also, he was going *two* and a half miles per hour.

No. Way. He was tearing it up over there. How was that even possible?

I looked at Leslee. "You know, it's not right when that guy can go faster than me."

She laughed. "I promise you'll be up to that speed in no time."

It felt embarrassing to know that I'd be beaten in a footrace by an octogenarian. For goodness sake, the night before my surgery I ran four miles of sprints at ten miles per hour. How could this happen to me?

The seven minutes passed slowly. Once again it was harder than I expected. I tried to focus on the view of the snow-capped mountains, but even the beauty of nature wasn't enough to keep my mind off the pain. I felt weak and shaky as I stepped off the treadmill. Leslee helped me to the recovery area and told me to stretch out and cool down.

Right. Cool down from my oh-so-strenuous leisurely stroll.

After I stretched, she took my final blood pressure reading and tested my oxygen levels. Then I was allowed to take off the sticky pads and return the heart monitor, and they declared me free to go. Before I left, though, Leslee grabbed a cardiac rehab t-shirt for me, which had a big pocket in the front to hold the heart monitor. That would at least let me feel a bit less like an invalid the next time I came in, so I was happy to accept it.

McCall helped me put on my coat. "How was it?" she asked.

"Ridiculous," I said. "The workout was silly, but it still kicked my butt."

"Don't worry," she said. "You'll kick its butt soon."

On the ride home, McCall remembered an errand she wanted to run. "Oh, Mom, is it okay if we stop by Target to grab a couple more strands of lights for the Christmas trees? Some of the lights we have aren't working. I'll pull up in front, and you can wait in the car so you don't have to get out. I know that workout kicked your butt." She gave me a teasing wink.

I laughed. The idea of going to the store actually sounded wonderful. "Sure. Actually, just park. I want to go in with you."

"Are you sure?"

"Yeah. I've got this. Didn't you see? I can do one point five on the treadmill."

We laughed again.

She parked close to the store, and as we walked in, McCall eyed the ride-on shopping carts. "Should I get one of those for you?"

I snorted. "Absolutely not."

"I shouldn't have even asked. How about a regular cart? That way you can hold onto it for stability."

"Yeah, that's probably a good idea."

With our cart, we slowly walked to the back of the store. For a few minutes, I enjoyed the bustle and activity of the holiday shoppers, but it quickly became overwhelming. The lights, the people, the packed shelves, the long lines—it was too much stimulation.

After we picked up the lights, McCall spent a few minutes browsing clothes, makeup, and so on. I watched her, glad that she had this chance to hang out at the store for a little while. She had to miss doing regular activities.

She suddenly stopped and looked back at me. "Oh, I'm so sorry, Mom. We should go."

I laughed. "Really, sweetie, just take your time." I tried to shut out my rising anxiety, not wanting to interrupt her brief reprieve.

"No, it's okay. I was done anyway."

We checked out and returned to the car. I felt wiped out, but there was a strange kind of joy at knowing I'd been able to go to Target. It's amazing how grateful you feel for the little things when you haven't been able to do them.

The following evening we attended the annual Christmas party at the house of my kids' Uncle Ryan. I spent most of the day resting and recovering from the previous day's activities. As night approached, McCall helped me get ready for the party. I'd lost all but a couple pounds of water weight, so I was able to put on real clothes. Hallelujah. So grateful for skinny jeans and sweaters, and for the wonderful ability to wear them.

The party was delightful, and my kids and I all had a great time. Dallin, Jace, and McCall all enjoyed spending time with their cousins and catching up. Everyone seemed thrilled to see me starting to look more like myself, and they said how grateful they were that I was there. I didn't feel great, but the ability to go out was more than worth the exhaustion it brought.

Despite the joys of the previous few days, the nights were still horrible.

That night, I woke up in the dark, my whole back throbbing all the way down to my tailbone. My upper back felt like every muscle and ligament had been ripped apart with pliers. Why weren't the pain meds working? I just wanted to lie down in bed instead of being stuck on the couch, but the last few attempts to do so hadn't gone well. Why was I in so much agony?

Well, duh, I thought. Probably from having my chest opened up, laying on an operating table for hours and hours, and not moving my upper body much for almost two months.

I felt miserable. I wanted to raise my arms up and stretch every muscle. In this state of mind, I couldn't laugh about my performance in cardiac rehab. One point five miles per hour? Who was I kidding? That wasn't a joke; that was just sad. Going into Target wasn't an accomplishment, it was something thousands of people did every day, and yet for me it was the highlight of the week. I felt pathetic. Why did this have to happen to me? Why me, and not someone who was already sick, someone who couldn't move around and was used to this sort of thing? Or someone who was better prepared for it emotionally? Or someone, anyone else? Out of all the people in this world, why me? And why did it keep going on and on? As another wave of pain rippled through my body, I thought, "Miracle or not, I just want to die."

With nothing else to do, I started to pray. "Father in heaven, please help me. Give me strength. *Please* give me strength to get through this."

McCall woke up and could tell instantly that I was struggling. "Mom, what can I do?" she asked.

"Nothing," I snapped. "There's nothing anyone can do. I just have to wait to get better, and I'm sick of waiting." I immediately felt bad for lashing out at her, and I started to cry. "McCall, I just can't do this anymore. I'm in so much pain."

McCall hurried to the nightstand. "I'm getting you another dose of pain meds. Please don't cry, Mom. It's going to be okay."

The extra meds took the edge off, though my back and tailbone still ached. McCall helped me change clothes, since I'd been sweating so badly.

After she settled me back down, she went back to sleep.

I stayed there on the couch and continued to pray. It felt sad that I couldn't even get down on my knees, but I knew Heavenly Father heard me either way. I pleaded for the strength to get through this and not let myself get discouraged. "I need to get better," I prayed. "I need to get strong again. I have so much I want to do. I'm so grateful to have this second chance at life, and I want to live it—really live!" I prayed about my love and gratitude for my three kids, who had been by my side for weeks. I thanked Heavenly Father for the support of my family and friends. And I continued to beg for the courage to persevere.

As I prayed, I felt a sense of renewed strength. Hard as it was, this was possible. I couldn't just feel sorry for myself. I knew that I could do hard things. The past five years had been full of them: ending a twenty-six-year marriage, raising teenagers as a single mom, a bout with stage three malignant melanoma, a heart attack, getting into shape, and of course all the challenges I'd already beaten on my journey to recovery. I could do this. I had to do this. I *would* do this.

The pain meds and prayers took effect, and I finally dozed off.

16
PROGRESS

Monday, December 10 – Tuesday, December 11

As the new week began, my mouth and throat finally returned to normal. Woo-hoo! I could eat and drink without any extra pain.

I also managed to stand up in the shower for a while. I even shaved and washed my hair on my own. I was a little shaky, so I moved slowly, but it felt great.

As McCall helped me out of the shower, I decided that I could finally look at myself in the mirror. The water weight was gone, the surgical cuts were healed, and I thought it was time to start accepting my new body. I stood in front of the mirror and studied myself.

I looked different. Since I'd lost the thirty-five pounds of water weight, what was left of me looked shrunken—almost like a skeleton. Most of my muscle mass, so hard-earned over the past year, had vanished.

McCall stood beside me. "I'm not used to seeing you look this frail, Mom. It's a little scary."

I agreed, but I didn't want to dwell on the negative. I'd made progress. That was what mattered. I cracked some joke and we laughed about it, brushing off what could have turned into a serious discussion. I'd had enough of those for the time being. I knew there would probably be more of them soon, today even, but for now, I felt more like myself than I had in the past month. I wanted to enjoy it.

At cardiac rehab that afternoon, I noticed a lot of elderly patients in the unit, some wearing oxygen, some barely able to move. As I walked on the treadmill, a heavyset older woman yelled, "If you have heart problems, we're all in trouble."

She chuckled, and I laughed with her. "Don't worry. I'll be out of here soon," I said. I hoped.

I was supposed to do eight minutes at my snail's pace. Sean, my physical therapist from when I was in the hospital, set the speed and left me alone for a while. After a couple minutes, I again noticed several of those older, sickly people moving faster than me. I felt silly. If they could go that fast, why couldn't I? Wouldn't I heal faster if I pushed my limits?

I glanced around and saw that none of the therapists were watching me. I could take the opportunity to test myself. I carefully set the speed up to two miles per hour (I didn't want to push myself *too* hard) and started walking a bit more normally. It was tough, but I wanted to see if I could do it. I looked back at the therapists, and no one had noticed. I smiled to myself and kept walking.

Sean returned shortly after. "How's it going, Teri?"

"Good." I held my breath, not sure if he'd realize what I'd done.

He glanced down at the treadmill readout and frowned. "Did you change your speed?"

"Er...yes," I admitted. Was it possible to get in trouble here? What would that mean? Surely he wouldn't demote me down to one or something, right?

He laughed and shook his head. I breathed a sigh of relief. Oh, good, he wasn't upset. "You're not supposed to do that." He checked my vitals as I continued at the increased speed, and after a moment of thought, he adjusted it back down to one point eight. "A compromise," he said. "Now leave it at this speed until you're done." He winked.

I grinned. "I'll do my best."

The treadmill time passed slowly, but I completed all of it and stretched out afterward, which felt wonderful on my stiff back muscles. They checked my vitals again and said they'd see me Wednesday.

I felt great about how I'd done. Once again, pushing myself forward had led to results. We stopped for a Diet Coke on the way home, which felt amazing on my now-healed mouth and throat. Ahhh. Progress.

***

On Tuesday, December 11, I had another appointment with Dr. Schorlemmer. McCall drove me there. The car ride was completely painless—no struggling with the vibrations of the car or the movement of the seatbelt. I still felt nervous whenever we came up behind another vehicle—painful or not, the airbag would probably undo all my accomplishments from the past months, and might still kill me. After so many steps in the right direction, the thought of losing my life to some silly fender bender terrified me. Fortunately we made it safely to the hospital.

We didn't use the valet. I walked in from the parking lot.

The receptionist and nurse both commented on how great I looked. At my normal weight, wearing normal clothes, with shaved legs and the ability to walk, I felt great. We joked and laughed about how quickly I'd shed the water weight—thirty-five pounds in four weeks. I felt like I'd made it through the worst.

"How is my miracle doing?" Dr. Schorlemmer stood in the doorway, smiling. His ever-present sunglasses sat perched on top of his head, and his reading glasses rested on his nose.

"I'm good," I said cheerfully.

He sat down on a stool and went over my chart. "How many times have you gone to rehab?" he asked.

"Twice."

"Hmm. I want you to be consistent with going three times a week."

"Oh." Between feeling embarrassed by my slow pace and the actual difficulty of the exercises, I had hoped to avoid going too often, but if the doctor said it would help me heal faster, I would obey. "Okay, I can do that."

"Good. Now, how are you sleeping?"

That was the one bane of my existence. Well, okay, not the one. There were several: the stairs, the couch, the bed, the lack of appetite, the difficulty of rehab. But sleeping was definitely near the top of the list. "I still can't lie down."

"Keep trying every day. I think it'll happen soon."

"Best news ever." Having fantasized about sleeping in my bed since I was first in the hospital, I couldn't wait to make it a reality.

Dr. Schorlemmer chuckled. "Just hang in there. Anything else you want to discuss?"

"One thing," I said. "I'd like to try driving again."

He hesitated. "Are you sure you're up to it?"

"I just don't like having to ask McCall or one of the boys to take me everywhere. Especially since I have to go to rehab so often." I hoped the mention of my rehab schedule would help convince him.

He thought for a moment and then nodded. "All right, I'll allow that if you can wait one more week. And you can do short distances only—no freeway driving. Just to appointments with me and to rehab. Deal?"

I considered that a win. "Deal. Thank you."

He smiled again. "This is a big step after a short time. You really are making an amazing recovery."

Today, I actually agreed.

I felt exhausted by the time McCall and I arrived home. I just wanted to lie down, so I hardly paid attention to what we were doing, even as we tackled the stairs. With McCall helping me, I kept putting one foot in front of the other and stubbornly ignoring the pain until I reached the top.

"Wow, Mom!" exclaimed McCall. "That was the best you've ever done."

I felt so sleepy that the importance of that moment didn't really hit me, but the accomplishment made me think that maybe I could sleep in my bed, too. Dr. Schorlemmer said it would happen soon. Why not today? That would make this day almost perfect.

McCall helped me to undress and lie down on the bed. I took deep breaths, trying to adapt to the pressure on my chest. McCall stood by and watched. "How does that feel?"

Deep breath in, deep breath out. I felt a dull pressure on my chest, but not too much pain. It felt like a Thanksgiving turkey resting on me, and not the whole refrigerator. "I think…I think I can do it." Deep breath in, deep breath out. I could do this. I *would* do this. Stay calm. Breathe. "Yes. I can do it."

"I'll be just down the hall if you change your mind."

"Okay. Thanks."

Deep breath in, deep breath out. Focus on breathing.

I fell asleep.

Oh glorious, heavenly sleep in my own, wonderful bed! Dreams of bright sunshine and golden seashores and peaceful, rolling tides. A full night of deep, healing rest.

That was what I thought would happen.

It was not what actually happened.

I wish that was the end of the bed saga, but I woke up just a few minutes after drifting off, suffering from the pressure on my chest. The metaphorical turkey had gained a few hundred pounds during those moments of sleep. It was too much. I had to get up. Sleeping in bed was one step forward that would have to happen another day.

I instinctively braced my arms by my sides to lift myself up to a sitting position. The second I tried to put weight on my arms, searing pain seized the middle of my chest, as if I had been stabbed. I gasped and fell backward, the wind knocked out of me. "Owww."

I lay still for a few seconds to regain my breath, and I remembered I still couldn't use my upper body. I had to roll over and roll up to get out of bed, without using any arm strength. It hurt, but I was able to do it. I slid off the bed and positioned myself back on the couch. Ugh. It felt better on my chest, but awful on my back and tailbone. I couldn't decide which pain was worse, but since my back hadn't undergone life-saving surgery, I decided it was safest to let that be the part to suffer.

McCall walked in a few minutes later, probably having heard me moving around. "Why are you on the couch?" she asked.

I sighed. "I just couldn't do it."

"Oh, Mom, I'm so sorry."

"It's okay, girl. It was better than the last try. I'll do it again tomorrow."

"I hope you can do it soon. I know how much better you'll sleep."

"I'll get there soon," I said. "I know it."

17
SOMEBODY TO LEAN ON

Wednesday, December 12 – Friday, December 14

Much as I wanted to start doing things for myself again, I continued to need the help of my family and friends. And goodness, did they come through.

I received a call one day from my friend Klistia. "Hey, Teri. Just FYI, I'm sending a cleaning lady over tomorrow to clean your house so McCall and the boys don't have to worry about it."

"That's so thoughtful!" I exclaimed. It would be nice to have the house cleaned, but I immediately felt guilty for what I thought was an imposition. "But really, we're fine. We can manage. You don't have to do that."

"Don't be ridiculous," she said. "I want to help. I'm having her come tomorrow. End of discussion. I'm sure you need it, especially with all that construction in your basement."

I thought about the ongoing project. Just two weeks before the surgeries, I had met with a contractor to finish my basement so that Dallin could move into it and save some money while he was finishing up at school. The construction had started the day before the trip to the ER. Very little happened on it while I was in the hospital, for obvious reasons, but we wanted it done by Christmas. They were now working every day—framing, sheet rocking, sawing, hammering, and so on.

Given the amount of dust that the construction kicked up, I concluded Klistia was right. "Okay, if you're sure," I said.

"Of course I'm sure. Just relax. I'll take care of everything."

Relaxing was never one of my strong points, but I could admit that I needed help in that area. "Okay. Thank you. I really appreciate this."

"Sure thing. You just get better."

"I will."

The cleaning lady arrived the next day. So did Klistia. She came up to see me and gave me a hug. "Hey, Teri. We'll have your house clean in no time."

"Wait," I said. "You're staying to clean, too?"

"Yeah."

"You don't have to do that."

She raised an eyebrow and smiled. "I want to. Just relax and let us help you."

I felt horrifically guilty the entire time they were working. I couldn't take care of myself, I couldn't take care of my kids, and I couldn't take care of my house. It had been almost two months, and I still depended on everyone else for the most basic of activities.

However, if they were willing to make such sacrifices for me, the least I could do was swallow my pride and accept it. I realized you never know the true meaning of humility until you're brought to your lowest point and see the people rise up to care for you.

Klistia came up later to tell me they were done. I cried as I hugged her. "Thank you so much."

She returned the hug. "You are so welcome. Just keep getting better."

What a blessing to have such amazing friends.

Another moment of humility came during one of my showers that week. I was able to take off my sweats and socks, but McCall needed to help me with my top. Dressing and undressing had become much less painful, but I was so tired of needing help for such basic activities.

McCall helped me into the shower and said she'd be back to check on me. I stood there, enjoying the warm water, until my legs became shaky and I had to sit down on the shower bench. My chest incision still felt very tender, so I washed carefully, shielding it from the stream. I felt very cold, which was strange because my body usually ran like an oven, so I kept adjusting the water hotter and hotter, enjoying the warmth.

Eventually I could tell I was running out of warm water, so I turned the shower off and called out, "McCall? I'm done."

Nobody answered. I frowned. "McCall? Is anybody out there?"

Still nothing.

I started to worry. Was she okay? Everyone was so busy worrying about me; what if something happened to one of them? I wouldn't be able to help, not as weakened as I was. "Hey! Hello?"

No response.

I began to shiver as a chill set in, and I decided I needed to go make sure everything was okay. I'd been receiving so much help. This time I could help myself.

I saw my towels hanging outside the shower door, so I pushed the door open and started leaning out toward the wall. Slowly, carefully, I reached out my hand, hanging onto the shower door to steady myself. Just a little further...a bit more...got them. My hand closed around the terrycloth and I pulled the towels into the shower to dry off. Yes!

I was shivering by the time I finished drying, and I had no idea how long I'd taken, but I sensed that it was a while. I slowly rocked myself to a standing position and wrapped the towels around myself, then gingerly stepped out of the shower. Water dripped behind me and left spots on the bathmat as I made my way over to the chair in the corner and sank into it, needing to rest before I made my way out to see where everybody was. I was freezing, and very fatigued, but feeling rather pleased with myself. I'd gotten out of the shower. One more thing I could do on my own.

I was just gearing myself up to walk out into my bedroom when I heard footsteps coming up the stairs. "Mom?" Jace called. "I'm home from work. You awake?"

"I'm in here," I called.

Jace came into the bathroom and saw that I was alone. "Where's McCall?"

"I don't know. I was going to try to look for her. I got out of the shower by myself, though."

He looked over his shoulder and yelled out toward the hallway, "McCall? Are you here?"

When my daughter didn't answer, I felt another flutter of worry. "Can you go see if she's okay?"

"Of course. Be right back."

Jace headed out, and I heard him wandering through the house looking for his sister. A few minutes later, he called out, "Found her!" Relief flooded through me. I could tell from his tone that nothing was wrong.

McCall came running in, her face white as a sheet and her hands fluttering in panic. "Mooom! I'm so sorry. I'm so, so sorry. After you started showering I went to lie down for just a minute in my room, and I must have fallen asleep. I'm sooo sorry."

"It's okay," I said, trying to calm her down. "Don't worry. It's okay. I'm fine."

She looked around and finally seemed to notice that I was dried off and sitting on the chair. "How did you get out of the shower?"

"Well, when the warm water ran out and I couldn't find you, I decided to do it myself." I smiled. "And I did. Piece of cake."

"I'm so sorry. I can't believe I left you in here."

"It's okay. It was a good thing. Now I know I can do it."

For a moment she couldn't seem to decide whether to laugh or cry, but she finally went with laughter. "I guess that's true. I'm glad you're okay."

"Me too, baby girl." We hugged. "But don't scare me like that again."

***

McCall drove me to cardiac rehab the next afternoon, since I still needed to wait the week prescribed by Dr. Schorlemmer before driving by myself. We'd had some snow, and the cold made my chest tighten with pain. It was going to be a bad day, I could tell.

At rehab, Leslee was the physical therapist on duty. She greeted me with a smile, which I only half succeeded at returning. After I hooked myself up to the portable monitor and checked in, she said I could go ten minutes on the bike and ten minutes on the treadmill. Last week I would have taken that as good news, but given the freezing temperatures and how tired I already felt, I just wanted to go home. The pedaling was hard. The walking was hard. Everything was too hard. I didn't want to be here. I wanted to finish with this whole recovery. I wanted to clean my own house and not have to celebrate getting out of the shower.

I somehow made it through the workout and went to hand in my equipment. Leslee paused and looked at me. "Are you doing okay?"

I felt like I was on the verge of tears, but I nodded.

"You're very quiet today."

I shrugged. "I'm fine. Just a little tired." I held in my emotions, not wanting to have a meltdown in front of the entire cardiac unit.

"Well, hopefully you'll feel a little better when we see you next."

In the car, I stared out the window as we drove home. People were out shopping for Christmas, working, and driving their kids home from school. They went jogging, walked their dogs, dropped mail off at the post office, ran to pick up groceries, went out to eat, and hung out with friends. They lived their lives.

Tears began to run down my cheeks as I realized my life had come to a complete stop. No warning. No time to prepare. Not even a traumatic incident to explain why it was so difficult. One minute I was a healthy, normal person; the next I was a heart patient who could barely get out of the shower on her own. Anger flooded through me, and I started to resent the people whose lives were untouched by this kind of tragedy. Why me? Why not one of them? They were out there as blissfully unaware as I had been the day before the surgeries. That Tuesday was an ordinary, regular day. And then everything went wrong.

McCall saw that I was crying. "What is it? Please don't cry, Mom."

I wiped my eyes. "Sorry, baby girl. I'm just mad about this whole thing. I just don't want to do it anymore. Three times a week with the rehab, the constant need for help…it's just so hard."

She grabbed my hand. "But you're doing so well. Don't get down about it. You can do this." She squeezed my fingers and repeated something I'd said earlier. "Piece of cake, right?"

"Devil's cake, maybe." She laughed at my joke, and I tried to smile. "Thanks for all the encouragement."

"No problem." We approached a fast food restaurant, and McCall pointed at it. "Hey, let's stop and get you a big Diet Coke."

My smile became genuine. "That sounds good."

"See?" She turned toward the drive thru. "It's the little things that keep you going."

***

The house smelled fresh when we walked in the door—a pleasant welcome. Climbing the stairs took more effort than usual. The dizziness was worse, and my stomach and legs cramped up something awful. I had to stop several times and bend forward to work through the pain.

We walked past my bed, and I wanted more than anything to climb in and bury myself in pillows and blankets. Since my chest was already hurting, though, I didn't try it. We headed instead to the couch.

My back and tailbone protested as I settled in, so McCall brought me something for the pain. I quickly dozed off into yet another restless sleep.

My growling stomach woke me up a bit later. I decided I wanted to go downstairs, and I contemplated calling someone to help me, but I felt pretty strong after resting. Going down the stairs was much easier than coming up. Maybe I could do it on my own.

Forget that. I definitely could do it on my own.

I got up from the couch and walked out past McCall's room. She was awake, and saw me as I passed the door. Her eyebrows rose. "Hey, where are you going?"

"Downstairs."

She hopped up. "I'll help you."

"No, I can do it. I'll hold onto the handrail. It'll be fine."

I expected more protests, but she must have known I needed to try this after the rough day. She followed me just to be safe, but I made it down the stairs with surprisingly little trouble.

I opened the fridge and stood there staring at it for a few minutes, something I hadn't done in a while. There was still a ton of food crammed inside, as people continued to bring meals over on a regular basis.

"Do you know what you want?" asked McCall.

"No."

"Keri's bringing dinner over in a bit. You could wait for that."

I shut the fridge. "That's probably a good idea. I get full too fast these days."

After dinner McCall helped me back up the stairs. As usual, it was awful. How could there be such a big difference between going down and going up? I groaned when we finally reached my room, and McCall asked, "Do you want to shower?"

"Yeah. I'm going to try to get out by myself again, though."

"Are you sure?"

"Yup. I've already done it, sleepyhead."

We laughed about how she'd dozed off the previous day, and McCall left me alone to try to handle the shower without assistance. I did well, managing to get out and dry off. As I sat in the chair afterward, I saw my pajamas on the counter, and decided to try to dress myself as well. The bottoms were no problem. The top was a button-up, so I didn't have to pull it over my head, though it hurt to twist around to get my arms in. After a brief struggle, I managed to get completely dressed without any help—another small victory.

The next day my friend Val hosted a Christmas luncheon in her home. Having been doing so well with my recovery, I really wanted to go. I wanted to get out and live, enjoying the holidays with the rest of the people in the world, the ordinary people I saw outside the car window.

McCall took me to the luncheon, and everyone gathered around as soon as I walked in. They settled me in a comfy chair, McCall went to get me a plate of food, and the rest of the party came to me so that I wouldn't have to move. Again I felt a bit embarrassed by how everyone was adjusting to meet my needs, but I quickly lost those concerns as I spent time with my amazing friends.

I realized that no matter what your struggle is, you need people around to lift you up and boost your spirits. To bring you food and help you climb the stairs. To encourage you when you just want to quit. It takes humility to admit you need help, but that help is what allows you to start standing on your own again.

18
ZUMBATHON

Saturday, December 15

One of the gestures that humbled me the most was when two of my friends, Laura and Lindsi, held a fundraiser to raise money for my astronomical medical bills. Lindsi taught Zumba classes, so the two of them organized a one-hour Zumba session at the gym where we all worked out. They made posters and flyers with pictures of me and my kids, posted about it on Facebook, and asked for fifteen-dollar donations from everyone who attended. They called it the "Bless Her Heart" Zumbathon.

When I woke up the morning of the event, I looked out the window, grateful after a long night to finally see light. My gratitude faded when I also saw a foot and a half of snow on the ground, with more powder falling from the sky. My stomach sank. With this kind of weather, I doubted anyone would show up to the fundraiser. My friends had worked so hard. I didn't want to see their efforts wasted.

I decided to attend anyway, despite knowing how depressing it would be if I got there and no one else came. At least I'd be able to support my friends for supporting me. McCall drove, and Dallin was going to meet us there, but Jace had to work. None of us planned on dancing, but we all wanted to thank Lindsi and Laura and anyone who attended.

Snow and ice covered the local roads, making the driving a bit treacherous. I squeezed the armrests until my nails dug into them, still afraid of what would happen to me if the car spun out and the airbag deployed.

"Mom?" McCall asked, glancing over at me in the passenger seat. "Are you sure you want to do this?"

I nodded. "Yup."

Snow plows had cleared the main roads, so once we left our neighborhood the driving was much easier. It finally stopped snowing, and we arrived at the gym just before nine o'clock, when the Zumbathon was scheduled to start. We headed toward the indoor basketball court, where the event would take place. I held my breath as we walked toward it, afraid of seeing a deserted room.

When I caught sight of the court, I stopped in my tracks. Tears filled my eyes, and McCall squeezed my hand.

It wasn't deserted.

A huge crowd was already there—friends, family, acquaintances, coworkers. It seemed like everyone I knew had come out. There were even people I'd never met before, who had heard about my situation and just wanted to support me.

And the people kept coming.

Even at full health, I would have needed to sit down. Fortunately there was a chair to one side of the court, so McCall helped me over to it and sat down next to me. Lindsi and Laura rushed around, making last-minute preparations. Friends who hadn't seen me since the surgeries came over to say hi. Most looked shocked at my appearance. I knew I looked like a shell of my former self, but everyone still expressed how grateful they were to see me and how much they loved me, and I thanked them for coming out despite the snow. Of course they all brushed it off as no big deal, but it was a huge deal to me.

At nine, Lindsi and Laura stood up in the front.

"Welcome, everyone," Lindsi announced. "Thanks for braving the weather to make it out here. We'll get started in just a few minutes, but I wanted to talk to you a little bit first." She talked about me and my medical situation. She also mentioned the Sandy Hook shootings from the day before. "Our hearts go out to all those families who lost their precious loved ones," she said. "In times of tragedy, people bond together and help those in need. It's through the struggles of life that we learn to lean on each other and come together as people. Today, we're blessed to be here to celebrate and support this miracle named Teri."

I started to cry again.

Lindsi looked over at me and waved. "She was actually able to come out here this morning, so I wanted to introduce her to all of you. Come on over here, Teri."

McCall helped me stand up, and I walked slowly to the front of the group, totally in tears. "Thank you," I blubbered. "Thank you all so much. Thank you, thank you, thank you." I put my hands on my heart—the reason all of this had happened—and bowed my head in gratitude. As I looked back up, I couldn't see a single dry eye in the crowd. They all began clapping and cheering, which made me sob even more.

I sat back down, and Lindsi turned on the music. Immediately the room became a celebration. Everyone in the Zumbathon danced their hearts out, and those who just came out to support us had a great time watching the dancers and chatting. Laughter rose from every corner, and my spirits felt higher than they had in a long time.

Laura came to sit down next to me. "Guess what? I counted the donations, and we're well beyond our goal! We set up a donation account on your behalf at the bank, so I'll deposit it there later today. This more than exceeded any expectations we had."

"Thank you so much." I felt like I'd said that a thousand times today, and yet still couldn't say it enough.

Laura gave me a hug and then went back to continue running the event.

As everyone left later that day, we said our goodbyes and thank yous. Everyone told me how much they loved me and how happy they were to see me here. I thanked Laura and Lindsi about a zillion times and gave them just as many hugs. Love and appreciation filled the air on both sides.

Christmas was drawing near. The warm feelings and sense of appreciation from the fundraiser warmed my heart and made me excited to see how my recovery would progress through the rest of the holiday season. Surely, with this many people behind me, I could conquer any challenges still in my way.

19
VICTORIES

Monday, December 17

Monday morning came after a longer, more miserable night than usual. I sat there, trying to adjust my position to give my aching back some relief, and sighed. "I can't do this anymore," I said to myself. "I can't sleep another night on this couch. I *won't* sleep another night on this couch." One way or another, I was going to spend the next night in bed.

My best friend from high school, Mary, had called and wanted to go to lunch that day. She offered to pick me up, but today was the first day I was allowed to drive by myself. I wanted to take advantage of it. I told her I could meet her at the restaurant.

I got myself off the couch just as Jace and McCall came in to see how I was doing. We chatted a bit, and then I made my way around to mentioning the lunch date. "By the way, I'm going to go meet Mary for lunch today. Just wanted to give you a heads up."

"Okay," said McCall. "I can take you over there and hang out in the area while you guys catch up."

"Actually," I said, "I'm planning to drive there myself."

McCall's jaw dropped. "What? No. No way."

Jace agreed, "Yeah, you're not doing that on your own."

"Hey." I frowned at them. "This is the first week Dr. Schorlemmer told me I can start driving. If he says it's okay, then I'm sure it's fine. Besides, I *want* to do this."

My kids shared a look of disbelief. "Mom," Jace said, "you're still having trouble going up and down the stairs. You can't just get in the car and drive somewhere with no build-up."

"At least do some practice runs around the block," McCall urged.

That sounded like what we had done when I was teaching each of them to drive. I could just picture myself slowly maneuvering around a three-point turn with my children encouraging me in the background. Even the idea of it made me flush with embarrassment. "I don't need practice runs," I said. "I've been driving for over thirty years. I remember how it works."

That was nowhere near the end of the discussion, but as they helped me get dressed, fix my hair, and put on some makeup, they reluctantly accepted my stubborn determination to drive myself.

McCall walked me to the car. She looked ready to cry. "Mom, *please* be safe. And call me if you need anything—anything at all. Jace and I can come and get you, and one of us can drive the other car home. So don't hesitate if you need help, okay?"

I kissed her cheek. "I will, baby girl. But don't worry. I'll be fine."

I strapped the seatbelt under my arm so it wasn't crossing my chest or resting on my incision. I took a deep breath, turned the key in the ignition, and felt the car rumble to life. The vibrations didn't cause any pain, which made me smile. I had this.

I backed out and drove out of my little subdivision, feeling a sense of elation with each movement of the car. Yes! I was driving. I had regained some of my independence.

As I turned onto one of the main roads, the traffic condensed, and I started to feel a bit overwhelmed. I also noticed a new tendency to drift toward the left side of the lane. I had to concentrate to compensate for it, which was weird.

I forced myself to stay calm. So it took a little more focus to drive. I could do this.

Fortunately the restaurant wasn't too far from home. I pulled into the parking lot, grateful and elated about my accomplishment. Mary met me inside, and her face lit up as she saw me walking on my own, dressed in regular clothes. Her expression clouded with that too-familiar sense of horror as I came closer and she saw how frail I looked, but she kept quiet about it. We hugged, chatted a bit, and then sat down to order. I told her everything about the surgeries and my recovery. We laughed. We cried. We hadn't spent much time together over the past few years, but it felt like no time had passed at all.

Before I knew it, several hours had flown by. I started to feel weary and decided I should go before I became too tired to make the drive home. Mary asked if I needed assistance, but I assured her I was fine.

Fortunately, I was. I made it home in one piece, though I was tired. Jace had gone out, but I saw McCall's car in the driveway. I pulled into the garage, unbuckled and climbed out of the car, and made it up the three little steps into the house without any assistance. By that point, I just wanted to crawl into bed and sleep, but I needed to go upstairs to do that.

"McCall?" I called. "I'm home." She was going to be so excited about how successful the drive had been.

She didn't answer, so I walked over to the stairs. I put my hand on the railing and yelled again, "McCall? Are you up there?"

Nothing.

My gaze fell on my hand, resting on the handrail, and followed the rail up to the landing. My eyes narrowed. Only these steps stood between me and my bedroom. I'd risen to one challenge today. Why not another? If no one was here to help me, I'd just have to climb them myself.

Breathe in. Breathe out. Breathe in. "You got this, girl," I whispered.

I lifted my foot. First step.

The first few steps were easy—I almost couldn't believe how hard they had been when I first came home.

On the sixth step, I felt the dizziness set in.

On the seventh step, it turned to lightheadedness.

On the landing, tiny bursts of pain crept into my chest and made it hard to breathe.

I started up the second flight, forcing myself to inhale deeply. My knuckles turned white as I gripped the handrail. Halfway up, I stopped and bent forward to relieve the pain in my chest and catch my breath. I looked up at those last four steps, and particularly toward McCall's bedroom door. If I called her now, she would probably hear me. She could help me the rest of the way. Three quarters of the stairs were enough for one day, weren't they?

I knew the answer before I even finished asking myself the question. No. They weren't. I wouldn't give up. I could finish this on my own.

I took another deep breath and continued putting one foot in front of the other. Fifth step. Sixth step. Seventh step. Breathe in. Breathe out.

Eighth step. As I stood there on the second floor, panting for air, my heart pounded half as much from pride as from exertion. My thoughts went wild. *I made it! I climbed those accursed stairs on my own. My biggest enemy lies defeated behind me. Take that, surgeries! Take that, house! I am Teri, and I can do anything. I'm a rock star!*

Okay, so I might have overreacted a little bit.

Once I calmed down, I went into my room and took my boots off. Then I arranged a bunch of pillows on the bed and stood staring down at them. I'd driven a car. I'd climbed the stairs. Surely I could handle lying down in a bed.

I slowly climbed up and situated myself amidst the pillows. Inch by inch, I lay back until I rested against them. I felt some pressure on my chest, but no real pain. I grinned. "You got this, girl," I whispered again.

McCall came in a few minutes later. I could tell from her rumpled hair that she'd been asleep. "Mom!" she exclaimed when she saw me. "When did you get home? How did you get up here? I told you to call me when you were coming home so I could help you."

I smiled. "Sorry, I forgot to call your phone. And when I got here, I didn't want to wake you up." My smile widened. "So I climbed the stairs by myself."

She sat on the end of the bed. "You did it? I can't believe it! And I feel bad that I didn't hear you come home."

"No worries." I started to laugh. "I can drive and climb stairs by myself. Your mommy is all grown up."

She rolled her eyes, but laughed with me. "And you're in your bed." she commented, patting the comforter. "Are you feeling okay in there?"

"Yeah, I'm good. Cold, though. Could you get me a blanket?"

She grinned. "Nope. You're all grown up. Get it yourself."

We laughed again as she retrieved the blanket for me.

As soon as she covered me, I fell dead asleep. I dreamed of the sweet taste of victory.

20
PRESSING ON

While sleeping in bed brought blessed relief to my back and tailbone, it still proved challenging. I couldn't yet roll to either side or use my arms to adjust myself, so I was stuck on my back. It wasn't painful, just uncomfortable. I felt restless, so the night dragged on, though it was nowhere near as awful as lying on that hateful couch. A couple times when I woke up, I glared at the couch and reminded myself that at least I was making progress. I never had to sleep on that horrible thing again.

Morning came with a chilly feel, and I craved the feeling of hot tea running down my throat and warming my stomach. McCall had fallen asleep next to me, and I didn't want to wake her up, so I rolled out of bed quietly and headed to the top of the stairs. I looked down them and smiled. I'd climbed up without help yesterday. Climbing down was always easier. I had this. I really had this.

I made it to the kitchen without too much effort and warmed up some water for my tea. After I steeped the teabag for a few minutes, I took a sip and felt the delicious warmth heating me from the inside out. What a wonderful, simple pleasure. I needed to take more time to appreciate those.

I envisioned the perfect morning spent sitting—not sleeping—on my little couch, drinking tea next to the space heater and watching The Today Show. Of course, to do that, I needed to climb back up the stairs. With a mug of hot tea in my hand.

Was this a bad idea?

Nah. I could do it.

I walked over to the stairs. I gripped the handrail with one hand and clutched my tea in the other. *One step at a time*, I thought. *You got this, girl.*

Step by step I made it up to the landing. Since it was the start of the day and I wasn't already exhausted, it was actually not as difficult as the previous night. I found myself smiling again as I climbed the second set. I shook a bit, and the tea jostled around in the mug, but I made it all the way to the top. Yes! Best attempt yet.

I walked to the couch, turned on the heater, and covered myself with a blanket. Then I flipped on The Today Show and sipped my tea. Ahh...paradise. I felt normal. I felt well. It was delightful.

McCall woke up. "Hey, Mom. Whatcha doin'?"

I raised my cup and chuckled. "Just sitting here and drinking tea."

Her eyes wandered from the mug, to me, to the hall with the stairs, back to the mug, and then back to me. "You...you didn't... how did you?"

I laughed. "Yeah, I did. I went down, made some tea, and came back up."

McCall leaped out of bed, a smile on her face. "Woo! You're crazy. I can't believe you did it. Great job, Mom."

A short while later, the lead contractor for the basement project came up to announce that the final inspection would take place today, the carpet would go in tomorrow, and then the renovation would be done. "Have you seen it yet?" he asked.

Throughout my recovery, I'd told him to just pick out what he thought would look best. He'd always been hesitant, but in my physical and emotional condition I hadn't been up to making those decisions myself. "No, but McCall has taken some pictures and shown me the progress. It looks great. I can't wait to see it in person."

The contractor smiled. "Well, as soon as we're done with the inspection, you can check it out."

"Thanks. I will."

Later that day McCall walked me down to the basement. We made it down all the stairs with no problem. The smell of new paint and the whir of fans filled the room. I turned around and around, surveying all the work.

Holy cow. It looked amazing.

I hadn't been down there since before the surgery, when the basement was completely open—no finished walls, just bare, cold cement. Now it included a family room, two bedrooms, a bathroom, and a nice storage room. I wandered from room to room, marveling at how well the colors matched and the quality of the craftsmanship. I loved the tile I'd apparently picked out for the bathroom—I didn't remember doing that—and everything the contractor had chosen looked great. The beautiful finished carpentry and custom closets were pleasant surprises. The colors were warm and inviting, and the big windows in each room made the whole thing feel bright and cheerful. I didn't remember the color of the carpet McCall had chosen, but from all of this I felt sure that it would look good when it was installed tomorrow.

When the time came for my cardiac rehab appointment that day, I drove to the hospital on my own, though McCall told me to call if I needed anything. She went out to run errands and do some shopping while I was out.

The traffic still made me uneasy, and I had to concentrate not to drift to the left, but I made it to the parking lot just fine. It was quite a cold walk to the entrance, and I began to shiver in my coat. Pain blossomed in my chest, and my legs and abdomen started to cramp up.

Oh no, I thought. *Do not do this now. Not after we've been doing so well. Come on, body, work with me here.* My limbs did not relent, which pissed me off. I really wanted to succeed in rehab today, after all of my accomplishments this week. It was just like my body to stop working right when I needed to show someone my progress.

A blast of warmth greeted me as I walked through the doors. I stopped shivering by the time I got into the elevator, and as I reached the third floor, I felt much better. I checked myself in to the cardiac rehab unit, greeted the enthusiastic therapists, and got started.

I was up to fifteen minutes on the treadmill and stationary bike. I felt pretty good about my progress. Finally I was outperforming the octogenarians on oxygen. I made it through the workout just fine. The therapists commented on my progress, and I felt like I would overflow with joy from how well I was doing. I called McCall and told her I was on my way home. As I drove back to the house, I felt good.

It was only one week until Christmas. How had it snuck up so fast? Whatever the case, I truly felt the Christmas joy today.

I went through the drive thru to reward myself with a Diet Coke. By the time I arrived home, I felt exhausted and hungry. I opened the fridge and browsed the mountain of leftovers inside. McCall came home a few minutes later, so I told her to sit down while I dished us both up some food. Of course she offered to do it for me, but I told her I was fine.

We sat down at the bar and talked as we ate. After we were done, I felt more exhausted than the previous two times I had climbed the stairs, but I still wanted to do it by myself. McCall followed me up just in case. My heart pounded and my legs shook, but I slowly made it to the top.

This was the first time she'd seen me do it on my own. As I bent forward to catch my breath, she clapped her hands and whooped like a cheerleader whose team had just won. "That was great, Mom! You did awesome."

"Thanks, girl," I said. "Hopefully soon I can do it without feeling like I'm dying at the top."

I showered that night while standing up the whole time. I dressed myself afterward, and decided to try brushing my own hair. I lifted my arm, and pain flashed through my chest. I stopped, then gritted my teeth. No, I didn't care if it hurt. I was going to do this.

I stubbornly ignored the pain and brushed my hair, then put it in a ponytail on the top of my head. As I looked at myself in the big mirror in my bathroom, I began to slowly raise my arms to see how high they could go.

I got them to shoulder height before the chest pain began. I pushed further. My torso throbbed as if someone was playing it like a snare drum. My arms began to shake. I finally had to stop. "Okay," I told myself, "tomorrow I'll go a little higher."

That had been the theme of my recovery—pushing to do whatever I could one day, and promising to do more the next. Finally it was starting to pay off. I knew that in just a few more weeks, I would be back to my normal self. I looked forward to returning to work, to exercising, running, skiing, and rebuilding the muscle I'd lost.

The days leading up to Christmas were busy. McCall and I went to a mall with Aunt Janice. My friend Wendy invited me for lunch and pedicures the day after that. The following day, Dr. Schorlemmer had me get some blood work done to see if what had happened to me was caused by a genetic condition. I wanted to make sure that this would never happen to my siblings or children, so I went to the hospital lab to get my blood taken before rehab.

I went eighteen minutes on both the bike and the treadmill. Piece of cake. I felt amazing.

Between all the activity, all the cardiac rehab, and all of my sudden progress in achieving things on my own, I thought I was nearing the end of this story. I'd cleared so many hurdles. Surely the end of the race was near.

21
CHRISTMAS

Saturday, December 22 – Tuesday, December 25

Just when I thought the race was nearly over, I found out there were several more laps around the track. I decided to go out and do some last-minute shopping to buy some fun gifts for my kids' Christmas stockings. I had a little money from all the generous donations we had received, and I wanted to do something for them after all they'd done for me.

I went to Target. The store was horrifically busy, so I didn't stay too long. I gathered a few stocking stuffers in sets of three and checked out.

As I walked out of the store, I felt a sinking feeling settle in my stomach. Where was I?

The area around me looked totally unfamiliar.

I turned and looked at the store, wondering if I'd left through the wrong doors, but I recognized the entrance. This was the right way to come out. I turned back to the parking lot, searching for my car.

I shivered in the cold and tightened my grip on my shopping bags. Oh no. Where did I park? More importantly, why couldn't I remember?

I started to panic. Why did I come to the store alone? What was I trying to prove? Now I was lost here, and if I didn't find my car soon, I was going to freeze, and who knew what that would do to my recovery? And what did it mean that I couldn't remember a place where I'd been not an hour before?

I resisted the urge to start screaming for help. *Calm down, Teri*, I told myself. *Just think. Try to remember where you parked. At worst, you can just walk through the aisles until you find the car.* For a moment I worried that I wouldn't recognize the car when I saw it, but I quickly pushed that thought aside. I knew what the car looked like; I just didn't know where I'd left it.

I took a deep breath and headed out into the parking lot, going in the direction where I thought I might have parked. I didn't see my car.

Okay, no need to panic. I tried another aisle.

Still nothing.

After a few minutes of wandering around, I finally caught sight of a familiar fender. Oh, thank goodness! There it was. I found it. Relief flooded me, and I hurried to load my purchases into the trunk and get into the car. I sat there for a few minutes, just breathing, scared by what had happened. What was wrong with me?

One thing was certain: I couldn't tell my kids about my outing. They'd be mad at me for going out alone. But at least that was over.

The next morning I caught the flu.

Fantastic.

I woke up achy and nauseous, so I made some tea to try to settle my stomach. McCall woke up, and as we chatted, I suddenly felt my stomach contents start pushing their way toward my throat. I headed to the bathroom as quickly as I could, dropped to my knees by the toilet, and violently vomited.

McCall ran in. "Mom, what's wrong?" She knelt and rubbed my back.

The vomiting sent flashes of pain through my torso, and I started to cry. Just when I thought I was finished, my stomach began heaving again.

"It's going to be okay," McCall said, continuing to rub my back. "It'll be okay."

This continued throughout the day. I tried to stay hydrated, but I couldn't keep any food down. Ugh. On top of being sick, now I was sick.

Fortunately I felt a bit better the next day, which was Christmas Eve. I rested most of the day, wanting to get over the flu before the Christmas Eve party at Uncle Ryan and Aunt Wendy's house. I recovered enough that I could attend. The party was wonderful, filled with games, photos, and fellowship. I even ate a little dinner. My kids enjoyed spending time with their younger cousins, and it was late by the time we left. We didn't want to go, but Santa would be coming soon. I smiled as I thought about the gifts I'd bought for my kids. It was worth the stress of the trip to the store.

When we got home, I gathered the stockings from the fireplace and took them to my room to fill them. I also wrote each of my kids a heartfelt note and put it in an envelope with some money, then returned the stockings to the mantle.

Christmas morning came. I woke the kids, and we all headed downstairs to the kitchen for our traditional Christmas breakfast. I cooked for one of the first times since my surgeries and loved every minute of it—churning hash browns, flipping eggs, and listening to the bacon crackle in the pan. We also had sausage, toast, and sliced fruit. The kids helped, and soon everything was ready to eat.

As we dished up the plates, the nausea returned. It wasn't as bad as the first day I was sick, but I couldn't eat anything.

After breakfast we all sat in the family room by the fire and opened our gifts. It was an emotional time, knowing how lucky we were to be gathered together that morning. There was an overwhelming sense of gratitude for how much our lives had been blessed over the past few months by our friends and family. All of the support, coupled with all of my recent progress, made us truly grateful.

I fought the nausea as long as I could, but eventually I needed to go upstairs to rest. I made it up the stairs on my own. Woo! Then I headed into my bathroom, and promptly started throwing up again. Boo!

It was bad. And it hurt a lot. I'd thought I was done with this kind of pain, but it seemed I wasn't as far along in my recovery as I thought.

I stayed in bed the rest of the day and had to skip the family Christmas gathering and traditional movie outing. My kids said it was totally fine, but I still felt bad.

So much for being better by Christmas.

Maybe by New Years.

22

A NEW YEAR

Tuesday, January 1 – Monday, January 7

I spent most of the next few days either sick in bed or throwing up in the bathroom. I slowly started to feel better, but I had lost another ten pounds. Normally a little flu wouldn't faze me, but in my weakened state, it took its toll. I looked like a skeleton. It freaked me out. I had been so unhappy about being overweight. Now I was distressed about being underweight. How could I go from one extreme to the other so quickly?

Fortunately, I recovered in time to bring in 2013. On New Year's Eve, one of my close friends had an open house for her daughter, who had been best friends with McCall since they were babies. She was leaving on an eighteen-month mission for the LDS church, so her family threw her a goodbye party. They lived about forty minutes away, but the drive went smoothly. Jace came with us, while Dallin had seen her earlier in the day.

Everyone looked amazed to see me. I couldn't figure out what the big deal was—why wouldn't I have come? I was on my way to recovery. Then I remembered how I must have looked. I didn't have the energy to put on makeup or do my hair. I wore leggings, a long sleeved shirt, and a baseball cap. My body was pale and fragile. It made sense that everyone would have that horrified, concerned look on their faces. I assured them all that I was fine, but I didn't think anyone believed me.

That night, at home, I tried to stay up until midnight to bring in the new year. The kids had gone out, so I climbed into bed to watch TV, but I drifted off. I woke up at about two am and realized I'd missed it.

I lay there wondering what the upcoming year held for me. What would my life be like? Would it ever be the same? What if I was destined to be this way forever?

No, nonsense. I'd be fine. Soon I would go back to work. I'd return to my former life, and all of this would just be a memory, a bump in the road.

New Year's Day was filled with football and family time. We sat by the fire, ate food, and hung out, anticipating good things for the coming months. I expected those things to start with my next cardiac rehab appointment the following day. I was up to a full twenty minutes on the bike and treadmill, and I was even doing some upper body strength training. I felt pretty good about myself and once more began brimming with optimism.

After my rehab appointment, I spoke to Leslee at the front desk. "I'm sure it won't be long until I'm running again. I see Dr. Schorlemmer next week, and I'm sure he'll give me the green light."

Leslee half smiled at me, though I could see some hesitation in her eyes. "You think so?"

"Sure. It's been like ten or eleven weeks by now. I'm sure I can go back to work soon, right?"

She shrugged. "For sure, ask him. We'll see what he says."

I didn't know it at the time, but she was humoring me. Maybe she saw how the positive feelings kept me going.

Over the next few days, I attended part of a hockey game, enjoyed a fantastic massage, and even managed to sleep on my side. I wrapped myself around my body pillow and found a position that didn't put strain on my chest. I almost shouted in victory. Nothing had felt better. After two and a half months, I finally felt like I was home. It was the best sleep I'd had since the surgeries.

I went into my work later that week to meet with HR. I only had a week left of medical leave, so I needed to discuss my return with them.

The receptionist jumped up in excitement when I walked in. She looked happy, but her face quickly clouded with that sense of horror everyone wore when they first saw me. I just wasn't the same athletic, sassy girl that had walked out of the office almost three months earlier.

She hugged me and began to cry. I thought my appearance actually scared her a bit. Laura had been giving them updates on my condition, but she was the only one to really see me since everything happened.

"We've all missed you," said the receptionist.

I smiled and tried to relieve her anxiety. "Don't worry. I'm fine. I'll be back soon."

My boss met me in the lobby. "Hey, Teri." He, too, had that look of concern. "We're meeting on the second floor. Do you want to take the elevator?"

I laughed. "Heck no. I used to give everyone crap if they took the elevator. What would they think if I took it now?"

We headed up the stairs. I felt a little lightheaded and shaky, which scared my boss so much that he started following behind me in case I fell. I made it up, though, and bent over to rest my hands on my knees.

"Are you okay?" he asked. "Do you need to sit? Do you want a drink of water? Anything?"

"I'm fine," I assured him. "No worries. I'll be back to my old self in no time."

I cracked a joke, he laughed uncertainty, and we headed into the HR office.

The head of HR did not have a concerned look; it was more like a what-the-heck-are-you-doing-here look.

We discussed my progress, and I told them I was sure I could return next week part time, and work up to full time within a few weeks. I told them I was doing great and making tremendous progress. By the looks on their faces, I didn't think they believed me. I repeated again and again that I was sure I'd be good to go after my CT scan and appointment with Dr. Schorlemmer in a couple of days. They asked about my physical activity and cardiac rehab schedule, and they said they hoped for the best. My boss insisted that I take the elevator back down.

I was actually grateful for that. I was feeling worn after the meeting.

But I was still sure I'd be okay to return to work the next week.

As I drove home, I couldn't believe how exhausted I felt. How long was I even there? Half an hour? Forty-five minutes? Why was I so tired?

Next week would be better. It had to be. I just couldn't take any more time off.

23
REALITY CHECK

Friday, January 4

I shivered as I walked into the hospital at eight thirty in the morning for the CT scan. By the time I made it through the front doors, I felt shaky and a bit angry. Why did I feel like this? It wasn't that long a walk. For some reason the cold made everything worse. I couldn't wait for spring.

I checked in and changed into a hospital gown. The technicians had me lay down and started an IV. They also covered me with a blanket—ahh, much better. The scan went quickly, which gave me time to stop by the lab for my blood work. It took a bit longer than I thought, and I was feeling tired by the time I finished. Originally I intended to go to cardiac rehab while I was there at the hospital, but the dizziness and lightheadedness got the best of me. I decided to just go home.

As I walked out to the parking lot, shivering and stiff, that sinking feeling crept into my stomach.

I couldn't remember where I parked again.

I walked up and down the rows of cars and felt the brisk air begin numbing my face and fingers. I bent over to catch my breath a few times and then kept walking. My footsteps quickened with my breathing as I searched. Where was it? Why couldn't I remember? This was ridiculous.

I finally pulled my keys out of my pocket and began hitting the lock button over and over as I walked. I finally heard my car horn calling me from a few rows away. Thank goodness. I walked over, hitting the button to sound the horn, until I found the welcoming sight of my own vehicle. Such a relief.

The seat warmer melted away some of my tension, but I still felt out of sorts as I waited for the car to warm up. Now this had happened twice.

What was wrong with me? What was wrong with my brain? I hadn't even finished with my physical issues. Was this going to be the next hurdle? I fought back worried tears as I pulled out of the lot and drove home.

Luckily no one was at the house at the moment; they were all either at school or at work. I closed the garage door while still in my car, and as soon as the door hit the ground, the tears began streaming down my face. I sobbed uncontrollably, sitting alone in the dark. This was too hard. It wasn't fair that I became tired after half an hour at the office or two tests at the hospital or a simple walk through the parking lot. I didn't care if it was a miracle I survived. I didn't want to put up with this anymore. I just wanted it to be over. I hated it. I hated my body. I hated what it was putting me through. This ordeal had to be almost over. I didn't know what I would do if it kept dragging on. Sure, I was a miracle, but I'd trade it all to just be normal.

Monday morning came, bringing with it my appointment with Dr. Schorlemmer. After so much discouragement over the past few days, I looked forward to it. Hopefully he would give me some good news that would get me back on my feet.

I drove myself to the hospital. I was getting used to the commute, between all the appointments and the cardiac rehab a few times a week. I just needed to remember where I parked this time.

The sun shone despite the cold weather, and I was able to find a parking spot close to the doors. I walked in and I chatted with the front desk women for a few minutes.

"You look great," said one.

"Yeah, the scar on your chest is doing amazing," said another. "That's one of the best we've seen. Most of them don't heal nearly as well as yours."

See? Encouragement. Just what I needed. I began to feel more secure that Dr. Schorlemmer would give me good news.

The nurse came out to the waiting area to get me and brought me into the back. She weighed me and noted that I was starting to gain back some of the weight I'd lost to the flu over Christmas.

"Is this your normal weight?" she asked.

"Almost," I said. "I need to gain about five more pounds." How weird to be eager to gain weight, after losing it had given me so much angst.

She took my blood pressure and went over my medication, and then the nurse practitioner, Andrea, came in. She gave me a hug, looked over my vitals, and discussed my progress, cardiac rehab, diet, and so on. About halfway through the conversation, I said, "I need to go back to work next week. Oh, and I want to start running again."

She gave me a funny look. When she saw that I was serious, she cocked her head and said, "Well, okay. I'll put that in the notes for Dr.

Schorlemmer."

The doctor came in a few minutes later, adjusting his glasses on his nose. "How's my miracle?"

As usual, I smiled when I saw him. "I'm doing great."

The nurse practitioner left, and the doctor sat down at the computer to look over her notes. "I just looked at your CT scan," he said. "Everything is healing great. Better than I could ever imagine."

I grinned. Good news, just as I expected! He started to talk about some other issues, but I didn't understand a word of it. I did catch him saying that I would need at least one more surgery to fix something, but that it could wait a while. Maybe even five years or so.

Whew. I couldn't handle the thought of going back into surgery any time soon. So far, it seemed that everything was looking up.

He read through the notes until something made him stop. He looked at me over the top of his glasses. "It says here that you want to go back to work."

I nodded. "Yes. It's been long enough, right? It's been almost twelve weeks. I figured that was enough time for me to at least go back to part-time. Oh, and I was also wondering if I could go running again? Of course I'll start slow, but I want to start putting my muscles back together. I feel like I can do it. I've been doing the bicycle at cardiac rehab, so I also thought maybe I could go to a spin class at my gym, to get back into biking. And maybe I could go skiing once or twice?"

He let me ramble on and on, not saying anything. He just watched me, not blinking, not moving. Just staring. I finally stopped talking, sensing that he had something he wanted to say.

He cleared his throat and scooted his stool closer to me. He leaned forward, folded his hands together, and looked me straight in the eye.

I knew instantly that I had everything completely wrong.

"Teri," he said in a very calming, yet matter-of-fact voice, "do you realize that you shouldn't even be sitting in this room right now?"

A chill rushed down my spine. I swallowed.

"You survived something that virtually no one has," he said. "There's no other surgery worse than this one. It's like being hit by a cannonball the size of Connecticut. You don't just get up and go back to normal after only three months. You've made unbelievable progress and I couldn't be more pleased. Yes, you have come a hundred thousand miles, but there's a million more to go. I'm not willing to take any chances with you. It's not worth the risk. It's not worth your life."

My heart sank. I sat there, listening and looking at him. As he continued to talk about my reality and what I'd been through, I felt my eyes swell with tears. This wasn't what I'd expected. This wasn't what I wanted. This was the worst news possible.

"Every couple months during this first year, I want you to have a CT scan to check the healing process," he said. "And I want to keep your blood pressure as low as possible. It spikes very easily, so it'll take medication, no stress, and a low activity level to maintain it."

I gulped. "How low?"

"I don't want your heart rate over a hundred beats per minute."

"W-what? Did you say a hundred?" How was I going to go back to work and start exercising again with that kind of limitation?

"Yes," he said.

"And did you really say a year?"

"Yes. At that point, we'll reevaluate, but I want you to take it slow. This is going to be a very long journey, but I'm here to help you through it."

My head spun. A year? No. No way. "How can it take that long? I can't do any of the things I love for a whole year?"

"You'll find other things that bring you happiness," he said. "Things you might never have known about. But this first year is very critical for long-term success. If you don't take it easy now, it will make it harder for you to go back to those things later. You need to trust me and take it slow. Let your aorta heal. If you do that, you'll probably have very few limitations on what you can do a couple years from now." He paused. "Except scuba diving. I would never take the risk of putting you under that kind of pressure."

I didn't want to go scuba diving, so that was an acceptable condition. But the part about years was not. This had to be a joke, right? "What about work?"

He considered. "I might be able to release you in a couple months to work one or two hours a day. But no more than that. You've been through a lot. You need to give your body time to recover."

One or two hours. That wasn't enough for me to keep my current job, especially not if it took two or three months to even do that much. I felt like I was drowning. I'd heard the thing about my recovery taking a year several times, but I'd blown past everyone's expectations multiple times already. They said, "You'll have to stay in the hospital until Christmas." I was out just after Halloween. "You won't be able to sleep in bed for a few more weeks." I was doing that now. "You should do some practice driving before trying the real thing." I drove out to lunch on my first try. I thought my whole recovery would be like that. The doctor's words didn't just take the wind out of my sails; they blasted gigantic holes through them.

What was I going to do? How would I pay my bills? How would I pay the huge amount I owed for my medical treatment? How would I live without my old hobbies? What would I do with myself? How was I going to survive?

Clearly I wasn't the same Teri who went to the hospital three months before. I might never be her again.

The question was: who was I now?

24
FROM THE JAWS OF DEFEAT

Somehow I set up my next appointment, checked out, found my car, drove home, and crawled into bed without completely breaking down. By the time I arrived home, though, I felt like a wreck.

Was had just happened? Was this real?

I really couldn't go back to work?

Would I ever be able to run or bike again?

Would I ever have another ordinary day?

I began to sob uncontrollably. I couldn't do this. I didn't want to do this. Hadn't I been through enough already? Why did I survive? Why didn't I just die? How was I supposed to hang on? Please, Heavenly Father, please let this be a bad dream.

Exhausted and drained, I fell into a deep sleep.

***

"How did your appointment go?"

It was a few hours later. I'd woken up and found McCall in my room. After a few minutes of chit-chat, she asked the obvious question.

I buried my head under the blanket.

"Mom? You okay?"

"Fine. Just tired." I started to sob again.

She came over and sat on the bed. "What happened?"

I told her about what Dr. Schorlemmer said, and how I wouldn't be able to go back to work or return to my normal life. She listened, nodding sympathetically, until I finished and dissolved into tears again.

"Mom," she said quietly, "I know how hard this is for you to accept…"

Oh no. With that start, I knew she was going to confirm what the doctor had said. I didn't want to hear it.

"...but this is what we've been told all along. They said from the beginning that your recovery would take a year, if not more. I know you didn't want to believe it, but it's reality."

I moaned.

"You're so lucky to still be here, though," she protested. "I know you can do this. Everything is going to be okay."

I tried to breathe normally, and I closed my eyes to make the tears stop falling. I didn't want to break down completely in front of her. I forced myself to repeat her words. "Everything is going to be okay."

I spent the next few days in my room. I didn't get dressed. I didn't go anywhere. I didn't talk to anyone. I didn't think about anything. I just couldn't face it.

I finally had to let my HR department know about my situation. That phone call was difficult, but I came out of it with some advice. They suggested I apply for disability and Medicaid, since I wouldn't have my health insurance through work anymore. That presented a whole new set of problems I hadn't even considered. I thanked the HR rep, and we ended the call.

I sat there alone, contemplating all the unanswered questions. I couldn't do the things I loved. I couldn't work. And apparently I was disabled.

How would I survive? How did one go about applying for disability? And what the heck was Medicaid?

I continued avoiding life for the next few days. The weather turned extra cold and gloomy, which didn't help my mood. I remembered the doctor talking about depression being a common symptom after such a traumatic surgery. I was on a small dose of an antidepressant, but it wasn't enough to pull me out of the dark completely. I fell into the void and didn't know how to climb out.

Looking back, it seems like I should be able to point to a moment, a particular time when I decided to fight back against the depression and not let it drag me under. But that moment never came. I never reached a moment of thinking, "Aha, I'm done with that now." It became a daily battle, just like the pain of sleeping on the couch. Just like every other struggle on this journey.

Every morning, when I woke up, I had the choice to succumb to that dark, hopeless place and stay in bed all day, or to get up, try to live, and keep putting one foot in front of the other. It wasn't an obvious physical challenge, like climbing the stairs or walking on the treadmill or sleeping in bed. It was my private, internal war with myself. My friends and family could support and encourage me, but the will to fight each day had to come from within. I had to find a reason to keep going.

I found one in my kids.

Each day, I decided to be strong. I fought for them, because they needed to see me fighting. They'd seen me beat life's mountains before, through a cancer scare, a heart attack, a divorce, and the loss of our house. The past five years were tough, but I'd gotten through them by taking one day at a time. Each time I had the choice to fight or give up. Only I could make that choice.

So I fought.

I applied for disability and Medicaid. I filled out the endless forms. I gathered information from my former HR department, my brother, the hospital, and my doctor. I went to the social security office and the state disability office. I saw the other people sitting in the waiting rooms, each of them going through their own struggle, which humbled me.

I kept fighting. I went to cardiac rehab three times a week. I went twenty minutes on the bike and treadmill and even started to work up a sweat. I pushed through each period of lightheadedness, dizziness, cramping, and medication side effects, and I slept when my body needed to sleep. I gave it what it needed to get better.

I engaged with my life as it had become. I went to a Jazz game with some friends who invited me, and I stayed for almost the whole thing. I attended my brother Wayne's swearing in as the new Utah Senate President. And I found new things to enjoy—things I could do in my present condition. I started cooking more. Dallin had been diagnosed with gluten intolerance, so I embraced the challenge of gluten-free cooking. I baked batches and batches of cookies and brownies, looking for just the right recipe.

I tried my best to live.

Some days were harder than others. Some days are still hard. But each time I chose to fight, it became a little more natural to choose to fight the next time.

25
OPENING UP

February

On occasion I may have fought a little too hard.

Based on how well I was doing in rehab, I thought it would be a good idea to start doing some things on my own. One day in February, the sun broke through the clouds and dried up the slickness of the roads and sidewalks. So I decided to go for a walk. Running outside during the cold winter had always been one of my favorite things—feeling the crisp air fill my lungs, seeing the snowbanks piled beside the roads, and enjoying the refreshing chilliness.

No one was home, so I bundled up, grabbed a beanie, gloves, my iPod, and my phone, and stepped outside. The sun warmed my face, and I closed my eyes and smiled up at it. This was what life was about. The quiet, simple pleasures of every day. Now that they were all I had, I learned to appreciate them more and more.

I shivered a bit, but I knew once I started moving I would warm up. I walked down the sidewalk and decided to follow one of the routes I used to run. As I passed out of my neighborhood, I noticed that I was having a little trouble walking straight. My body felt off-balance, and I tended to drift to the left. It took real focus to stay in the middle of the sidewalk. I actually started laughing at myself and this new, weird quirk.

I climbed a small hill and started to feel the lightheadedness set in. The wind picked up, and I had to stop and bend over as a cramp began in my legs and abdomen. I took a few deep breaths, and the cramp cleared away.

Ha, I thought, *take that, body.* I decided to keep pushing myself.

I turned a corner and realized I had an even bigger hill ahead. Ugh. I forgot about that. The wind now blew into my face, and I shivered as the sun passed behind a cloud, darkening the entire area. But I kept going. I started my chant from when I was just beginning to walk in the hospital: *I. Can. Do. This. I. Can. Do. This.* I focused on putting one foot in front of the other, keeping my eyes fixed on the grey sidewalk ahead.

Victory tasted sweet as I made it to the top. Yes! I grinned at my achievement, despite shaking with weakness and cold. I turned to look at the way I'd come and...

Froze.

Oh no. What had I done?

All this time, I'd been walking further and further away from home, never stopping to think about how I was going to get back. Now here I was, a solid two miles from the comfort and safety of my house, alone in the wind and freezing weather with no mode of travel except my own legs, and those were about to give out. My whole body shivered and screamed with pain, and I couldn't fathom making the return trip.

Embarrassed and a little scared, I pulled out my phone. I was afraid to call one of my kids. They'd be furious with me for coming this far out by myself. But I was desperate.

I dialed McCall's number.

"Hey, Mom."

"Hey, baby girl. Um, where are you?"

"Just leaving work. Why? Are you okay? You don't sound good."

I paused. "I, uh, I went out for a walk. And I can't make it home."

"You did *what?*" As expected, I could hear the shock, fear, and anger in her voice. "Where are you?"

Another pause. "By the Sandy Amphitheater."

"That far? What were you thinking? You need to know your limits! You're straight-up crazy!"

"I'm sorry. I just didn't think it was..."

"I don't want to hear it. I'll be there as soon as I can. Stay put."

I shivered there for a few minutes, both longing for McCall's car to appear around the corner and dreading the well-earned tongue lashing I was sure to receive. When she pulled up and I climbed in, I sighed with relief as the warmth of the car started defrosting my body. "Thank you so much, baby girl," I said. "I'm sorry."

McCall didn't look at me as she began driving me home. "I'm so mad at you right now," she said, shaking her head. I could see her jaw muscles clenching as she fought to contain herself. "I don't even want to talk to you. Do you realize you're two miles from home?"

"I'm so sorry," I whispered.

Tears pooled in the corners of her eyes, though she still wouldn't look at me. "You could die out here in the cold. Do you get that? Imagine what that would do to all of us! Don't *ever* do that again!"

We rode the rest of the way home in silence.

After climbing up the stairs and taking a hot shower, I felt physically much better, but emotionally I wasn't sure how to make it up to my daughter. I suspected she'd spent the whole time thinking about what I'd done, and I felt awful for scaring her like that. Truth be told, I'd scared myself, too.

A few minutes later, McCall came in, and I wasn't sure what to expect. But instead of continuing the fight, she came over and gave me a hug. I could tell she'd been crying.

"I love you, Mom," she said, burying her face in my shoulder. "I'm sorry for yelling."

I returned the hug, glad that everything was okay. "Don't worry about it," I whispered. "I love you too. Thanks for saving me today."

She sniffled and tried to laugh. "When are you going to realize you can't do stuff like that?"

"I realize it a little more each day."

***

In early February I received a phone call from the marketing director for St. Mark's Hospital.

"We're doing a commercial promotion for St. Mark's and Mountainstar Healthcare. We're taping individual interviews with patients who have received treatment there, and we're having them share their stories. Your name was given to me as someone I should definitely talk to. I don't know anything about your story, but they said you're a miracle. Would you be willing to go on camera?"

"For real?" I asked. "You want to hear my story? I'm not even fully recovered yet. I'm still going in for rehab."

"Yes, we'd love to hear it, if you're willing," he said.

If what I'd been through could help the hospital that had saved my life, I wanted to do anything I could to support them. "Okay, sure. I'll do it."

"Great. We'll email you all the details. Feel free to call me if you have any questions. I'll see you in a few weeks."

After giving him my email, I hung up, still trying to process the fact that my story was big enough news to put on TV. I called some close friends and shared my excitement with them. Maybe this would help people. Maybe this was why all of this had happened. They all shared my enthusiasm and told me to go for it.

A few hours later, enthusiasm faded to fear as I realized that talking about what happened to me would involve—gulp—actually talking about what happened to me. My emotions had risen and fallen like storm waves throughout my whole recovery. Could I really handle this? I didn't even understand the total nature of my surgeries. Dr. Schorlemmer had explained it several times, but I didn't grasp a lot of it, especially some of the medical jargon. Plus, every time anyone tried to discuss it, I became overwhelmed. And this was with my family and the man who saved my life. How was I going to sit in front of cameras with a bunch of people I'd never met and tell them my story without crying through the whole thing?

I called the marketing director back. "I need to know how you're going to interview me. What's the process?"

"Sure," he said. "It'll be shot in black and white. I'll sit in front of you and ask questions, but you'll be the only one on camera."

"Can I get a list of the questions?" I thought if I could rehearse my answers, it would help me not break down when I had to repeat them for the tape.

"We're not prepping any of the people we interview. We want it to be raw, real, and unrehearsed."

Well, if my interview went the way I thought it would, he'd definitely get some rawness. I just wasn't sure anyone would be able to understand what I was saying through my weeping.

"Don't worry," said the director. "You'll do great."

I certainly hoped so.

The weather turned bitter over the following weeks, creating the coldest winter Salt Lake City had seen in twenty-five years. I did my best to stay engaged with life. I had lunch with friends in my home, went to rehab and my medical appointments, and even went back to Bunco for the first time since October. Before I knew it, the day of the commercial shoot arrived.

Luckily I was scheduled for the afternoon, because I took a long time to get ready. I dressed in real clothes, did my makeup and hair, and drove myself to the studio. McCall had planned to come with me, but she'd been hired at a new job and had to work.

I made careful note of where I parked, then walked into the studio and waited in a little lobby. A production assistant came in carrying a clipboard. "Hi," she said. "What's your name?"

"Teri Benson."

She checked the clipboard. "Okay, Teri, follow me. I'm going to take you back to hair and makeup."

Wow. They had someone doing hair and makeup? They were really going all out with this. I hoped I lived up to their expectations.

We entered a room with a vanity, bright lights, and a big mirror. The counters were covered with cases of makeup and hair supplies. A lady was just finishing the makeup on an older gentleman. She put the finishing touches on his face, told him he was ready to go, and then turned to me.

"Have a seat," she said, smiling. "You look great. I won't have to do much with you."

The compliment made me smile. I sat down, and she began adding color to my eyes and concealer under them.

As I sat there, the marketing director walked in. "Hi, Teri, I'm Mark. We spoke earlier on the phone. It's great to finally meet you."

I thought about the cameras, and butterflies fluttered through my stomach. "I'm super nervous," I admitted.

"You'll do great," he said. "Just relax. I'll see you inside once you're finished here."

Mark headed back to the filming area while the makeup artist touched up my hair. "All right, you're ready. You look beautiful," she said.

"Thanks." I smiled, shook her hand, and then followed the girl with the clipboard back to where they were filming.

There was a big, plain backdrop set up, with a stool positioned in front of it. The older gentleman from earlier was sitting on it, with four cameras set up at different angles around him and people manning them. Lights shone on him from every direction, with those black umbrella things set up behind them to point the light in the right direction. Mark sat on a chair about four feet away, directly in front of the man. I could hear them both talking, just like they were having a regular conversation. Ten to fifteen crew people were working and moving around the set, talking on headsets. The whole thing felt very professional.

The clipboard girl took me over to a food table and told me to help myself if I wanted anything. I laughed. "Thanks, but I'm way too nervous to eat."

A few minutes later, they finished with the older man, and then it was my turn. Mark helped me sit on the stool in front of the backdrop and then took the chair in front of me. I felt my heart racing, and I tried to stay calm.

"We'll be talking for about an hour," Mark explained. "The cameras will be going the entire time. Don't worry if we need to stop at any point. We'll edit two commercials from this—one about thirty seconds, and the other will be two or three minutes. I'll ask you questions, and they'll film your answers."

I took a deep breath and nodded. "Okay."

"The cameras are rolling, so let's get started." Mark began the interview. "What you had was an aortic dissection, correct? Can you explain what that is?"

His relaxed demeanor immediately made me feel more comfortable. This would be okay. I gave him a quick overview to the best of my ability, though I didn't feel like I really understood it all. Even the gist of my explanation was enough to make everyone in the room take on serious expressions.

"Wow," he said. "You really are a miracle."

"That's what I'm told," I laughed.

"Okay, first question," he said. "How did you know this was happening? Were you sick? Was it painful?"

I reflected back on that ordinary day, October 23, 2012. "No," I said, shaking my head. "It started with just a little chest pain…"

I proceeded to tell them the whole story.

***

When the interview concluded, the room was dead silent. I looked around and saw tears on many faces, and I wiped away the ones on my own cheeks. I'd been emotional through the whole interview, but for the most part I kept my composure.

Mark stood up and came over to me. "Thank you so much for sharing this with us. You did an amazing job."

"Thank you," I said. "It feels good to talk openly about it."

"How long ago was this?" he asked.

"Four months this week."

His eyes widened. "Whoa. That's still so fresh for you. All of our other interviewees are at least a year out from their experiences."

"Well, I'm just taking it one day at a time." I looked around the silent room again. All eyes were on me, and I could tell they were all thinking somber thoughts. I decided to try to lighten the mood. "Hey, don't worry, everyone. I was just kidding. I made all that stuff up."

It broke the tension. Everyone laughed, and they began setting up for the next interview.

Once we finished, everyone told me it was a pleasure to meet me. I thanked them for making me feel so comfortable. I felt truly honored and glad to have been able to do this, and I hoped it would help others who may have gone through similar trauma, as well as promote the hospital and the surgeons who saved my life. I drove home feeling happy, if exhausted.

I had plans later that week to meet with Brandy, one of the nurses from my operations, to spend an afternoon together. Strangely enough, she was at home for a few days recovering from some minor heart surgery, so we thought it would be a good idea to hang out.

Feeling emotionally strengthened from talking about my surgeries during the interview, I decided to ask Brandy to explain to me the details of what really happened that day.

I was finally ready to face it.

26
UNDERSTANDING

Friday, February 22

My heart pounded with tension as I sat across from Brandy on her living room couch. This was it. She was going to lay it all out. I was going to learn the whole truth.

She took a deep breath and faced me, fixing me with her piercing brown eyes. "First of all," she said, "do you realize what a miracle it is that you're still alive? I honestly can't believe you're sitting here talking to me today. Are you sure you're ready for this?"

I nodded. "Yes. Tell me everything. I want to understand."

"Okay." She paused, and then began. "I woke up at four thirty that Wednesday morning to get ready for work. I was supposed to be at the hospital at six a.m. for a full day of surgeries. Just a couple minutes after I woke up, my phone rang.

"I saw it was Dr. Schorlemmer, and I knew instantly that it was bad news. Otherwise he would never call at that hour. If there was an emergency cardiac surgery, he'd send out a mass text to the team. He only spent the time to call when he needed his very best people. So I knew it was very, very bad. He said, 'Get here as soon as you can. We have an aortic dissection.' I thought, 'God, help us save this one.'

"I hurried to the hospital. I knew it would be an emotionally difficult day. Usually in these types of situations, my stomach does somersaults and I have a sinking feeling in my heart. I mean, losing a patient is always tough, especially since part of my role is to be there to support the family and friends. But for some reason that morning, I didn't have any of those thoughts. I wasn't worried. I didn't think anything in particular about what was coming. I just got to the hospital, prepped myself, and went to the

OR."

Brandy swallowed. "That's when I saw you. You were upset. You were scared. Crying. You looked up at me, and…" Her voice caught for a moment, and she paused before continuing. "You said, 'I know you. You're Brandy, Karla's daughter-in-law.' I couldn't remember where I knew you from, and I freaked out, trying to figure it out so you wouldn't feel bad. Then you said, 'I made the bridal jewelry for your wedding five years ago.'

"Suddenly I recognized you, and the operation ahead became much more personal. I didn't want to worry you, so I tried to calm you down and told you everything would be okay. I said we were going to take good care of you. And then the anesthesiologist came in, and it all began."

As she trailed off, I reached out and squeezed her hand. Since I didn't remember most of this, I was sure it was much harder for her to talk about it than it was for me to listen. However, I knew what was coming next would disturb me. I breathed in, breathed out, breathed in. "Go on," I said quietly.

"Your aorta had torn in the arch, which is the worst possible place for it to tear. It had torn down to the root. You were put on the bypass machine, which keeps the heart and lungs working without blood flow during most open heart surgeries, but they couldn't use that for you just yet. So they shut the pump off and cooled your body down to sixty-four degrees Fahrenheit, basically freezing you."

I blinked at her. "Freeze me? How did you do that?"

"The anesthesiologist packed your head and neck in ice, and then the perfusionist shut down your heart and circulatory system. It's called circulatory arrest."

My circulatory system? The system that kept blood flowing through my body? Holy crap.

"They brought in this thing called the slusher, which is kind of like a Slurpee machine. It makes an ice solution, which we packed around your heart to preserve it."

"That sounds awful," I whispered.

"It was. It brought on the pressure, too. From the time your body temp hit sixty-four degrees, Dr. Schorlemmer only had a forty-five-minute window to do the repairs needed so you could go back on the bypass machine for the rest of the surgery."

I frowned. "Why was that so important?"

Brandy looked at me seriously. "No one wakes up after forty-five minutes. Not ever. If he couldn't do it in that time, it was over."

My heart stopped for a few beats. I hadn't realized just how close to death I really was.

"Even then, we wouldn't know what other damage had been done from the lack of oxygen. Brain damage, organ damage, collapsed arteries…it could have been awful. But Dr. Schorlemmer works well under pressure. In my fifteen years on the cardiac team, I had never, ever seen him sew someone up that fast and precise. He was done in twenty-five minutes."

I tried to crack a joke. "Twenty to spare."

Brandy didn't laugh. "Teri, you had no blood flow or oxygen. You were straight-up dead for twenty-five minutes."

Okay, she was right. It wasn't funny.

She kept going. "After that, we put you on the bypass machine and finished the surgery, which took about ten hours. But we lost you two more times during that. Your right ventricle shut down, and we had to stop the surgery to revive you."

Excuse me. What. *What?* I died *three times* and still survived? How was that even possible?

"After that we started warming you up and took you to ICU to finish returning to a normal temperature. And then all that was left was praying. We all prayed so hard that you would just wake up."

I could tell from her tone that there was more to the story. I couldn't imagine what else was coming.

"On Friday morning, the doctor called us in because your colon, kidneys, and liver were in failure. The main arteries had collapsed. We knew you wouldn't survive without another surgery to repair them, but we weren't sure you could survive the surgery itself, either. We also had no idea how bad the damage was, and it was possible you'd have to have a total colostomy or be on dialysis for the rest of your life. We..." she hesitated. "We weren't sure it was worth it.

"We all sat around a table and waited for Dr. Schorlemmer's decision. After fifteen minutes or so, he finally said, 'We're taking her back in.' It was supposed to be a two or three-hour surgery, but it turned into seven or eight." Brandy shook her head. "I was in awe. Dr. Schorlemmer did procedures I'd never even seen before. He's a genius, Teri. It was incredible. And when he was done, the failing organs began to function like nothing had even happened."

I had to remember to breathe. I knew I owed the doctor my life, but only now did I realize just how big that debt was. I started to cry.

Brandy wept with me, but she smiled through her tears. "You were far from out of the woods, but we all had high hopes. Dr. Schorlemmer is the best surgeon for this type of procedure. The best in the entire mountain west."

I wiped my eyes and asked, "How many aortic dissections did he do last year?"

Brandy's voice was quiet when she answered. "I don't know the exact number. There are different types of dissections, and some aren't as life-threatening as others. But we had about five of the type-A kind last year, and yours was the very worst of them because it had gone into the root of the aortic valve and was leaking."

Breathe in. Breathe out. Wow. No wonder my recovery was taking so long.

And then Brandy hit me with the biggest bombshell of all. "You were also the only one of those five to survive."

The dam broke. Tears streamed down my face. "Really?" I blubbered.

Brandy looked at me, tears staining her own cheeks. "It's true." She nodded. "You truly are a miracle."

***

As I drove home from Brandy's house, I felt afraid. What had happened was bad. Really bad. I was dead for twenty-five minutes? How was that possible? And my heart had stopped two other times? What did all of that mean? This was all so scary. I wished I could just go back to the beautiful place and curl up in safety and…

Wait. Most of the time the beautiful place was out of reach. The only time I had really been there was during the surgeries, and it was only for a few minutes. Maybe about twenty-five minutes?

Oh. Oh my.

I had been in that place because I was dead. I couldn't get back there now because I was alive.

I thought of that place, with its indescribable beauty and complete absence of pain, and it really sank in. I had died. And I came back.

Three times.

I'd heard over and over during the past four months that I was a miracle.

Now I truly understood why.

***

Knowing about my miraculous survival really put things in perspective. October 23, 2012 could easily have been my last day. That was it. Nothing after it. No more me. I'd woken up to another ordinary day, going through the motions, with no idea that I was about to die. It could have all been gone in an instant.

It made me realize that, for the past ten years, I'd been living in survival mode. I was just getting by. I was alive, but I wasn't living.

There was so much more I wanted to experience, so much more I wanted to do: seeing my kids graduate from college and get married, holding my grandchildren, seeing a Broadway show in New York, running in Central Park, seeing the world from my bike, sitting on a beautiful beach, somehow inspiring and helping people. Before the surgeries, I'd felt like there was something more I was supposed to do with my life, but I wasn't pursuing it. If I hadn't survived, I'd have lost the chance forever.

I couldn't repeat the same mistake.

I often thought about the beautiful place. As much as I missed its peace and purity, I knew I was where I belonged. I had my life here on earth, and it was my job to do something with it. So each day I woke up and tried to take another step forward. Unlike the first part of my recovery, though, I wasn't trying to return to the life I had before. Instead I tried to make the most of the life I had now.

I started doing my cardiac rehab at my own gym, where I used to work out. I wore my heart monitor and took my blood pressure. I walked on the treadmill and rode the stationary bike and did very small amounts of light weight training. I kept my heart rate under a hundred beats per minute. I learned to work with my new body instead of fighting its limitations. I started seeing a chiropractor to help with my back pain. I spent time with my kids. I took each day at a time. I appreciated each moment.

Sure, my body was weaker. I couldn't go back to work. I couldn't exercise. I couldn't do a lot of the things I wanted to do.

But I could still *live*. I could enjoy the magic of every ordinary day, because there was no telling which would be the last.

27
ROUND TWO

March – April

I had another CT scan at the end of March, followed by an appointment with Dr. Schorlemmer the next week. My mood was upbeat as I headed to the appointment. It had been almost six months, and aside from the side effects of my medications, I felt good. I was happy with my progress. I was learning to accept my new self.

I chatted with the girls at the front desk and then followed the nurse into the back. "You look good," she said as she checked my weight and vitals. "Are you having any problems?"

I grinned. "Nope. Everything is going great."

"That's wonderful!"

"Yeah," I agreed, still smiling. "It really is."

Dr. Schorlemmer came in, happy as ever, with his signature sunglasses perched on his head and his reading glasses down on his nose. "How are you doing, miracle?"

"Great," I repeated. "I'm doing well with the rehab. I'm able to get around the house by myself. I can go out and run errands when I need to."

"Excellent." He looked over my records on the computer screen. "You look amazing, and you're doing amazing. Better than I ever expected, as usual." He chuckled. Then his expression sobered. "However..."

Uh-oh. I didn't like how he said that. Something bad was coming.

My newfound optimism tried to push away my worry. I'd survived being dead. How bad could this be?

"I looked at the CT scan you had last week," he continued. "I see a couple of areas in your aorta that aren't getting the necessary blood flow to heal properly. And you need another graft. Here, I'll show you."

I scooted my chair over so that I could see the screen. He started the video of the CT scan and pointed out the problems. I didn't quite understand, but I did my best to follow along.

As the video concluded, he said. "I'd like to get this done as soon as possible, but it can wait a few months if that works better for you."

I spoke slowly, working my way through what he was telling me. "You're saying I need another surgery?"

"Yes."

I must have looked like I was going to have a panic attack, because he hurried to add, "It wouldn't be a complete open heart surgery. Just a small incision."

Flashbacks of the horror of my early recovery flew through my mind: sleeping on the accursed couch, climbing the stairs, the smallest tasks becoming insurmountable chores, being unable to clean myself, feed myself, take myself to the bathroom.

All of my optimism did a swan dive out the window. I couldn't do that again. I couldn't. No, no, no, no, no.

"I really don't think I can handle another surgery," I said quietly.

"I promise it will be nothing compared to the magnitude of what you went through six months ago," the doctor said. "Really. You'll only need a week or two to recover."

Even a week or two of going through that torment again felt like more than I could bear. "I just don't know…"

He patted me on the arm. "You can go home and think it over. Just call the office on Friday and let them know when you want to do it. They'll take care of all the setup."

Friday. That gave me about a week. It was too long and too short at the same time.

As I left his office, I felt numb. Somehow I walked to my car and drove home. No music. No sound. Just me and the silence.

I arrived home to find McCall in the kitchen. I walked in, looked at her, opened my mouth to tell her the news, and started bawling.

"What's wrong?" She rushed over and started rubbing my back. "Mom, what happened?"

"I…I need to go in…for another surgery."

"Oh no!"

Tears filled her eyes, and we cried together.

Eventually we both calmed down, and McCall began reassuring me. "I'm sure it'll be okay, Mom. Dr. Schorlemmer knows what you need. You can do it."

"I'm not ready." I wiped my eyes. "I can't go through that again. Maybe I'll wait until the end of summer."

"Are you sure that's safe?"

"I'm not sure of anything. Well, except that I don't want anyone to know about this yet. I'll tell the boys, but no one else for now, okay?"

"How long will you have to be in the hospital this time?"

That wasn't an agreement with my request, but at the time I was too distracted to notice. "They said just a few days."

McCall thought for a moment. "Maybe you should just go in and get it over with."

"Maybe." I felt exhausted, and I didn't want to talk about it anymore. "I'm going upstairs."

I cried myself to sleep. I'd thought I was finished with doing that.

***

I told Dallin and Jace, who both took the news pretty well. They joined McCall in saying that Dr. Schorlemmer knew what was best for my recovery. My brain knew they were right, but my heart was afraid. Even the thought of going back into surgery made my chest ache.

I tried to ignore the whole thing the next day. McCall and I were going shopping with my friends Lindsi and Klistia. We all piled into Lindsi's car and headed to downtown Salt Lake City. I decided to just have a good time and think about the problem later.

That was until McCall said out of nowhere, "Hey, guys, my mom has a little bad news to tell you."

The car went silent. I whipped my head around to stare at McCall with a very dirty look. "I don't know what you're talking about," I said, trying to cover.

"What is it, Teri?" asked Lindsi.

"Yeah, what happened?" said Klistia.

"It's nothing. I don't want to talk about it."

"Teri, you have to tell us. Otherwise we're going to worry all day."

Ugh.

"It's really nothing. I just, I found out yesterday that I have to..." My voice became small. "...go in for another surgery."

Questions came flying. "What?" cried Lindsi.

"Why?" asked Klistia.

"When?" Lindsi continued.

"Add 'who' and 'where,' and you'll have the full set," I grumbled. "I'm not doing it until the end of summer. It'll be no big deal."

"That's not what you thought last night," McCall said quietly.

I ignored her. "Really. No worries."

"Why didn't you tell us?" Lindsi asked. "We're here for you. Seriously."

"I know. I just didn't want to worry you."

"Teri, stop it." Lindsi rolled her eyes. "We're going to worry unless you tell us how you're doing, so just tell us what's going on. You're ridiculous."

Klistia and McCall and even I had to laugh in agreement. She was right. I wasn't doing anybody any favors by keeping it all to myself. "Thanks," I said.

The encouragement started immediately. "You're going to be fine. I'm sure this surgery will be way easier than the last one," Klistia said.

I smiled as I heard Dr. Schorlemmer's words repeated by someone else. "Yeah. You're right."

And that was it. Everyone felt so confident about my ability to recover that we didn't worry about it for the rest of the day. The shopping trip continued as planned. I even forgot to be mad at McCall for bringing it up. If I didn't think about it too much, maybe it wouldn't feel like a big deal.

***

I flip-flopped a million times about when to do the surgery before I finally made a decision. Part of me wanted to wait until I felt completely better—which I was sure would happen at the end of the summer—before subjecting my body to another ordeal. Another part just wanted to get it over with. I was home. I wasn't working. If I did it now, I could enjoy the summer without another surgery looming over my head.

I woke up Friday morning and made the call to Schorlemmer's office. When the receptionist answered, I told her I had decided on the end of April.

"Okay," she said, "the first surgery time available in his schedule is Friday, May third. Will that work?"

I looked at my calendar, even though I knew I had nothing scheduled. "Yes."

"All right. I'll set that up. You'll have a pre-op appointment two days before that for a chest x-ray and blood work."

"Thanks."

I hung up wishing that this wasn't happening.

I let a few more friends and relatives know about the scheduled surgery and tried to put it out of my mind.

Spring arrived over the weekend, bringing beautiful warm weather and the promise of fresh flowers and brighter days. I could feel the pall of winter lifting from my shoulders, and I started to feel hopeful. I'd gotten through the night. Now it was the morning. I just had one more hurdle to overcome. This would be fine. And I had until May to get ready for it. Two weeks was enough time to prepare emotionally. Everything would work out.

On Monday morning, my phone rang.

***

"*This Friday?*" I practically screamed into the phone.

"Yes," said the receptionist, taking my reaction in stride. "Dr. Schorlemmer has an opening, and he wants to do it sooner rather than later."

"I can't come in on Friday," I answered reflexively.

"Why not?"

"I, uh, I don't know. I just can't. I'll find a reason later."

"So…you *are* available Friday?"

I sighed. "Yes."

"Okay. I'll schedule you in, then. I set up your pre-op appointment for Thursday at one o'clock. Just check in first with radiology."

"Uh-huh."

I felt brain-dead through the rest of the conversation, and by the time we hung up, I wasn't completely sure what had happened. What the heck? I was having the surgery in four days? How did that get set up?

Before panic could set in, I tried to think rationally. This way, I was just getting it over sooner. Less time to worry. This was a good thing.

Right?

***

I went in for my pre-op on Thursday, April 18, after three days of trying my hardest not to think about the surgery and praying incessantly for perseverance. The appointment went well, and I was reminded again of how miraculous my survival was. I saw the x-rays of where Dr. Schorlemmer had grafted my entire aorta—something the technician had never seen before. I marveled at the images. For the first time I could see something that before I had only felt.

I began to feel calm. I was being watched over. This would be okay. The peace I'd been praying for descended on me like a cozy blanket. I'd go in, be home in a couple days, and most of the people in my life would probably never even know it happened. So I thought.

Later that day, my phone buzzed with a text message. "Teri, just wanted to say we're praying for you."

It was from someone I didn't remember telling about the surgery, but maybe I'd just forgotten. "Thanks," I sent back. "Feeling good about it. I'll be fine."

A few hours later I checked my phone again and discovered half a dozen texts. What? Where did these come from? They all wished me the best and conveyed prayers and good wishes for my surgery. I also had a bunch of emails and voicemails, all expressing their support and love. Just like after the first surgery. But how did they all find out?

Oh no. No, she didn't. She couldn't have.

"McCall!"

I hurried to the computer and logged on to Facebook. There on my page, for everyone to see, was a post saying that I was going in tomorrow for my third heart surgery. I hadn't written it, so I knew McCall had been the one to share the news.

So much for keeping it quiet.

I remembered that my daughter was out, so I dialed her cell, punching the keypad with way more force than necessary. When she answered, I shouted, "You posted the surgery on Facebook again!"

I heard her take a quick breath. "Don't be mad, Mom. I just wanted everyone to know so they could pray for you. They want to be supportive. And after everything they've done for us, I thought they deserved to know." I could hear tears threatening in her voice. "Please don't be mad."

I stopped to collect my thoughts and my emotions. *Breathe in. Breathe out. Breathe in.* So my privacy had been broken. Now everyone knew about my upcoming ordeal. The Facebook post only led to outpouring of encouragement, so why was I so upset about this? I knew what was coming. I had to face it, too. McCall's actions forced me to accept that. I couldn't hold that against her.

Besides, she was right. These people had been there for me when I needed them most. They'd probably be hurt if I hid this from them. I owed them honesty. I couldn't be selfish about this. *Breathe in. Breathe out. Breathe in.*

I chuckled a bit, trying to relax. "I was really mad at you," I said, "but you did the right thing."

She exhaled in relief. "Thanks, Mom. I love you."

"Love you too, baby girl."

"You'll see," she said. "This will be a breeze."

***

I arrived at the hospital at six thirty. I changed into the gown and the socks with the grippy things on the bottom. McCall put my clothes in the white hospital bag. The nurses took my vitals and put in an IV line. It all felt eerily familiar.

I was allowed to walk to the operating area, which was encouraging. After a while, Dr. Schorlemmer came in, and I brightened, feeling some of my anxiety fade. "The man has arrived!" I declared to the room at large.

He laughed. "Are you ready?"

"Yes. Let's do this."

He briefly explained the procedure, though I didn't understand it any better than I had understood the first surgery. Given how scary I found the description of the first one, I figured it was best that I didn't completely know what was going on.

We chatted with the anesthesiologist as everyone prepped for the surgery. The nurses all buzzed around, commenting on how great I looked, how well I was doing, and how easy this procedure would be. I still felt nervous, but I continued to pray and remind myself that this was just a follow up to what I'd already been through. Everything would be fine.

They started the anesthesia, and before I knew it, I was out.

***

A beeping sound filled the room, pulling me out of sleep. More familiar noises chimed in—humming equipment, the muffled sound of nurses outside the room, the clicks and whirrs of various machines.

I opened my eyes. I was in the hospital, in a bed, in the ICU. And I was still here.

My friend Laura was sitting in a chair by my bed, as my kids hadn't been able to change their work schedules to accommodate the sudden surgery date. "Hi," I told Laura. My throat didn't feel raw like it had before, so that was a good start. "Thanks for coming."

"Hey." She beamed at me. "Welcome back. They said everything went great. It took less time than they thought. How are you feeling?"

"Pretty good. Just sleepy. Much, much better than last time."

A nurse came in, and I repeated the conversation with her. The nurse asked, "Is there anything I can get you?"

I hesitated. "My throat's dry. Can I have some ice water?"

Remembering the torturous thirst I'd experienced the first time, I was afraid she'd say no. But she immediately nodded. "Absolutely. Be right back."

Thank goodness.

I carefully took an inventory of my body, checking in with each part of myself to see what hurt. To my surprise, I didn't feel too battered. There was a small, two-inch incision in my groin area, but my chest itself felt okay. I pulled the neck of my gown up and looked, and there wasn't even a cut there. Apparently this had been much, much less invasive. I wondered how that had worked as I drifted off to sleep.

Between my naps, McCall and the boys all checked in on me, and McCall said she'd let everyone know that I did great and would be home in a couple days. Dr. Schorlemmer stopped by shortly after that and confirmed that I had only needed the small groin incision, and that I would be here in ICU tonight and tomorrow, but then I could move to a regular hospital room and maybe even go home on Sunday.

The night dragged by, what with the noises and frequent checks of my vitals, but during the following day I was moved to a regular hospital room in the cardiac unit. Yet again, it felt familiar—very small and cozy. But my activity level was far different. I could get up and move around with ease. I went for walks around the nurses' station with no help—a far cry from the pain-filled days after the first surgery. With each thing I managed to do, I felt more and more encouraged that this recovery would indeed be a piece of cake.

They let me go home the following day, and Dr. Schorlemmer said he'd see me in two weeks. I dressed myself. I walked out to the car—no wheelchair needed. I enjoyed the spring sunshine on my face rather than the biting cold from the past November.

McCall drove me home, and we met the boys at the house. Despite this surgery being far less invasive than the first ones, there was a mountain of goodies on the kitchen counter—food dropped off by friends and family to keep us going while I recovered. Again I felt a flood of gratitude for all of the people who loved us.

I wanted to lie down and go to bed, but I hesitated as I remembered the agony of walking up the stairs six months ago. Fear gripped my heart— what if that happened again? If this recovery was going to give me problems, climbing the stairs would definitely be one of them.

Stop it, I told myself. *You're doing fine. Just go upstairs, take a nap, and stop stressing about it.*

I gripped the handrail, lifted my leg, and climbed the first step. And the second. And the third. And so on, all the way up to the top. No problem.

I was grinning by the time I finished. This was a definite one-eighty from the last time.

My room contained several beautiful flower arrangements from loved ones, giving me both a welcoming view and another rush of gratitude. I climbed slowly into bed. My whole body felt a little stiff and sore, especially where the incision was, but not enough to complain about, especially not in the shadow of what came before.

I felt overwhelmed by happiness as I lay in bed and drifted off to sleep. This whole recovery would be simple.

This time, I didn't feel like I was in denial.

28
EMBRACING THE EXTRAORDINARY

April – June

Five days after the surgery was the six-month mark since the original incident. Wow, I thought. It had really been six months? Six months since that plain, ordinary day. Six months of yearning to get back to normal. To not have limitations. To work. To run. To ride a bike. To have energy. To do all the things I wanted to do. To have another ordinary day.

As I thought about those ordinary days, I realized they were also meaningless days. They had no purpose. They were just…ordinary.

I didn't want ordinary anymore. My recovery had made me realize that I wanted a different life. There was a reason I was still here, and I wanted to live up to it. I wanted to give people hope that this life was just a small part of our existence. That what lay ahead would bring happiness beyond our wildest dreams. I had seen the extraordinary in that beautiful place and in the miracles that happened to keep me alive. I wanted to bring that experience into the regular world.

One night, just as the late news ended and the commercials began to run, I was surprised to see myself on the TV. My commercial for the hospital was playing. I sat there on the stool in front of the backdrop, talking about my experience and how the surgeons had saved my life. I watched it, intrigued, and realized the commercial wasn't embarrassing at all. They'd done a great job editing it, and the whole thing looked very professional. I came across as a brave survivor, and I thought I did a good job of conveying how grateful I felt toward the doctor, nurses, and hospital.

A few minutes later, the phone rang. I saw Jace's number on the caller ID, so I answered. "Hey, what's up?"

"Hey, Mom." His voice sounded a little strange.

"Are you okay, Jace?"

"I'm fine. We're watching the NBA playoff game. We just saw…" His voice cracked, and he cleared his throat. "We just saw your commercial. It was really good."

Aww. I smiled at how touched he was. That meant a lot to me. "Thank you."

He wasn't done. "We're all in tears, Mom. I called you because all my buddies wanted me to tell you how amazing and inspiring you are."

My eyes watered. Jace was twenty-two, and his group of friends were all around the same age. Touching the hearts of a group of early-twenties boys was not an easy thing to do. It meant so much to me that my experience had impacted them in this way—had made them stop, consider their lives, and feel grateful for what they had. It was just a taste of the power of what had happened to me.

"Thanks for sharing that with me," I told Jace, wiping my eyes.

"I love you so much, Mom."

"I love you too."

Bringing the extraordinary into the ordinary—that was what this was all about.

Sometimes that was easier said than done. Dr. Schorlemmer told me I needed to take it easy for the first couple weeks after the surgery. I took that to mean a few days. But as the month of April came and went, I didn't recover as quickly as I anticipated. I went outside to enjoy the spring weather and go for a walk, and I discovered that the stamina I'd so painstakingly built up was gone. I couldn't walk far without horrible fatigue and pain.

A week after the surgery, the swelling in my right leg and foot hadn't gotten any better. The right leg was also the leg where I'd had my lymph nodes and a huge chunk of my thigh removed after cancer was discovered there in 2008. It now looked like the remains of a shark bite, but it hadn't given me any trouble for years. I couldn't figure out why that side of my body had swelled when Dr. Schorlemmer went in for the surgery through the other side.

Maybe I shouldn't have gone in. Maybe I should have waited. I'd been making so much progress, feeling so much better, finally connecting to my purpose, and then it was back to square one. Well, okay, not completely back to square one. I was in much better condition than in November. But I still felt annoyed by the setback.

As frustrated as I felt each day, I was determined to get through it. I hosted Bunco thirteen days after the surgery, and it went well. We had a family get-together on Mother's Day, and I had a wonderful time with my kids. They all expressed their appreciation for me. McCall said that Mother's Day would have "totally sucked" without me there.

At my three-week appointment with Dr. Schorlemmer, I tried to be my usual upbeat self, but I admitted my frustration. He explained that even though the incision was small, there was still a lot of internal trauma. I had to be patient and let my body heal.

"Yeah, but what about all this swelling in my right leg?" I asked. "It's ridiculous."

He took a look at my bloated foot and leg. "Well, it doesn't look that bad. I've seen much worse."

"What? Are we looking at the same leg? It looks like a water balloon."

"In comparison to your other leg, it does look very different, but medically it's not that bad," he said, far too rational for my liking.

"Why not?" I insisted.

"You don't have any lymph nodes in your right groin, so the ones on the left have been doing the work of two. Now that they've been compromised by the surgery, it's causing some lymph fluid issues on the right side. The lymph system is very delicate. It might take a while, but your body will sort itself out eventually. Just give it time."

"Ugh." I flopped back on the exam bed.

He chuckled. "If you want to do something to help it along, you can wear a medical-grade compression sock and keep your leg up as much as possible. But I know you won't like that suggestion."

"No," I agreed, "I don't." It was almost summer. I was not about to wear a compression support sock in the middle of the heat. "Thanks, though."

"No problem."

He concluded the appointment by telling me how pleased he was with my progress, and he said he was very hopeful that I wouldn't have to go in for a fourth surgery. In eight weeks he wanted me to have another CT scan to see how everything was responding. I hoped I'd at least have two matching legs by then.

I slowly began to get my strength back. By the time six weeks had passed, I saw great improvement in my strength and stamina. With the summer in full swing, I wanted to be outside as much as possible, so I began to walk more, going further and further from home. I even went on a few hikes up in the mountains, though I always wore my heart monitor. I even went four-wheeling with a friend one weekend. I wasn't sure Dr. Schorlemmer would have approved that outing, but I had an amazing time.

My bike had been sitting in my living room since the last time I rode way back in the fall—a lifetime ago. The day finally came when I could go for my first ride since the surgeries.

My friend Julie came to the house with her bike on a sunny Saturday morning. We weren't going too far or too fast, since I needed to keep my heart rate under 100 bpm. When cycling, I always wanted to push faster and faster. I knew I had to focus on keeping my heart rate down.

We brought the bike outside, and as I mounted it, uneasiness crept up on me. The balancing requirements felt unfamiliar, and my grip felt foreign on the rubber handlebars. I clipped one foot into the pedal, which made my heart quicken a little—I had taken a few spills in the past by not being able to un-clip my feet fast enough to stop.

"Are you okay to do this?" asked Julie, watching me struggle to get ready.

"Yeah," I said. "I've got this."

I clipped in my other foot, and we were off.

I shook a bit as I got started, but we rode slow. Despite riding in the bike lane, the passing traffic still made me nervous. Gradually, though, I began to find my rhythm. My balance improved. My ride became smoother. I didn't shake while stopping and starting at intersections. I picked up the pace of my pedaling.

It felt *so* good. I hadn't realized how much I'd missed this until I returned to it, feeling the wind rush by my face, gripping the handlebars and feeling the bike respond to my every command, becoming one with the movements of pedaling and steering, flying down the road with the grace and speed of a rushing river. It was exhilarating, and I loved every second of it.

Grinning widely, I glanced down at my heart monitor to see how I was doing, and I nearly crashed.

Holy crap. It read 120.

I stopped pedaling immediately. What? How could that number be right? I wasn't even working that hard.

We continued the ride granny-style, going at a slow, measured pace. I watched the monitor like a hawk, not willing to risk complications by losing my attentiveness again. Even at the slow speed, it was difficult to keep my heart rate down. This stressed me out, which of course sent my heart rate even higher. The rest of the ride was a balancing act between productivity and safety, and it drained my mental energy considerably. By the time we returned home, I felt nothing but relief to be done.

As much as I loved being back on my bike, the stress and fear overshadowed the enjoyment. It just wasn't fun when I had to be so cautious.

Julie and I sat on the porch and drank glasses of water as we talked about the ride. "It'll get easier," Julie assured me. "You're doing so great. You'll be back riding in no time. Just not yet."

I smiled. "Yeah. Soon." I wanted to believe her, but I had a bad feeling that this would take a lot longer than "no time."

I took my bike back inside and parked it in my living room, where it had sat unused for the past eight months. I left my shoes, helmet, gloves, and riding sunglasses next to it. I didn't know when I'd use them again. It was possible that this part of my regular, ordinary life wouldn't be a part of my future.

Despite feeling called to a greater purpose, sometimes I missed the ordinary.

29

NEW LIFE

July – September

By the first part of July, the snow had finally melted on the high mountains. One afternoon when Jace was home, I asked him to go hiking with me.

He thought that sounded like a great idea, so we drove up Big Cottonwood Canyon to a ski resort and picked a hike we'd done before. It started with an immediate uphill stretch, but I thought the rest would prove doable and would make up for the difficulty of the start. The smell of pine and the sounds of birds lifted my spirits and made my heart soar with anticipation. How I loved the outdoors.

As we began to climb, I realized I had forgotten something. "Jace, I think I left my heart rate monitor at home."

He stopped immediately. "I'll go back and get it."

"No, wait." I shook my head. "I'll be fine."

His face clouded. "Mom…"

"I know, I know. But really, I'll be fine. I'll go slow. I promise."

He hesitated a bit longer, but finally relented and continued with me up the hill.

The steep grade proved waaaaay longer than I remembered, as did the hike as a whole. We stopped to rest regularly, and I felt fatigue setting in, but the breathtaking mountain views and the beauty of the clear day kept my mind off of it. It felt so good to be out, to be able to move, to be alive.

Other than the wind rustling through the trees and our footsteps on the path, nothing broke the peaceful silence. My mind wandered back to that beautiful place, with its scenes of majestic color and its deep sense of serenity. I felt like I belonged there, that I was home. I felt some semblance of that on the hike, and it made me reflect on all I had been through.

Nine months ago I had been lying in the critical care unit, fighting for my life, surviving something almost un-survivable. Now I felt my lungs fill with the clean forest air, felt my heart beating as I walked, and felt the joy of being out in nature.

Nine months ago I could barely stand. Now I could hike multiple miles on end.

Nine months ago I felt like the stairs to my bedroom were a mountain. Now I stood atop an actual mountain.

Nine months ago I wished I hadn't survived.

Now I treasured the second chance I had been given.

We stopped to gaze over a sparkling lake. I felt the weight of all I had been through resting on my shoulders. I carried it with me, and I knew I would carry it for the rest of my life. But today it didn't feel like a burden. "I believe in miracles," I whispered.

Jace looked over at me. "What, Mom?"

I smiled at him. "Nothing. Let's keep going."

And going and going and going. For as long as I was meant to be on this earth, I would keep going.

***

I had another CT scan at the end of July. Dr. Schorlemmer said my progress was continuing incredibly well, but that he still wanted me to be cautious. He decided we should wait until January to review any potential changes in my lifestyle, instead of clearing me for more activity in October.

Three extra months. I took the news in silence, and my heart sank a bit. Even so, I knew that if anyone knew what was best for me, it was him. I nodded. I smiled. I said, "Okay."

I kept going.

Reality could sting, but I was learning to be the new me.

***

I spent five days at Bear Lake toward the end of the summer. The last time I'd been there was my fiftieth birthday—only ten months ago, though it felt like a lifetime. I had biked fifty miles around the lake to celebrate.

I brought my bike on this trip. I wanted to ride, even if only for a little while. I cruised slowly around the paved trail to the marina, making a conscious effort to keep my heart rate under control. I wanted to speed off with no limitations, but of course I didn't. I accepted my new self. I enjoyed it as much as I could, and I enjoyed the memories I had from previous visits here. I wasn't the same person as I had been then, but at least I could still make new memories.

A few days later, I spent time with my family at the lake. McCall somehow convinced me to go out on a paddleboard, something I had never tried before. I climbed up and knelt on the board in the shallow water, focusing on keeping my balance. I began paddling out from the shore. It didn't seem too difficult, so I decided to try to stand. As I got to my feet, wobbling and shaking like crazy, I nearly toppled over, face-first into the lake. Somehow I regained my balance, and I paddled toward a line of buoys floating some distance out from the beach.

I still tended to veer toward the left a bit, but I was so shaky on both sides that it didn't make much difference. I made it there without falling off, so I turned around and started back, still standing and feeling pretty proud of myself.

The water became shallower as I approached the shore, until it was only about five inches deep. I prepared to step off the board in triumph, holding my paddle above my head like a conquering hero, when a small wave suddenly hit me from behind. I pitched forward, bounced off the board, and crashed into the shallow water, right in front of a beach full of people.

Ow.

I picked myself up, feeling places where I was sure I was going to bruise, and looked toward McCall. I just knew she was going to be furious with me for standing on the board in such shallow water. *Mom, you could have killed yourself! You have to be more careful.*

When I spotted her, though, she wasn't running toward me in a panic or staring at me with a look of disapproval. She was laughing.

She was laughing so hard that *she* fell over, too.

I made my way to her. "So, that was dignified," I joked.

"Absolutely," she agreed before dissolving into giggles again. "That was one of the funniest things I've ever seen!"

"Glad I could entertain you." I stuck my tongue out at her before sitting down in the warm sand and joining her in laughter.

And a new memory was made.

***

Summer saw me growing stronger, walking more and doing some light weight training. I hiked as much as possible. I went to concerts, weddings, and barbecues, loving every moment. My birthday arrived on September 1, and while I had previously hated birthdays, now I enjoyed it immensely, truly appreciating what it meant to be alive.

As the weather cooled and the leaves began to change to red and gold, I was able to start working a bit. The regimen of going to work stabilized my life, even though it was an adjustment physically. I loved it, and I needed it.

The year moved into October, and I found myself looking at my calendar from the previous year. I looked at what I was doing in those weeks prior to October 23. Those last few days should have been precious, but instead they were routine. How different would things have been if my life had ended on that operating table? I found the date of my last bike ride. The last day I saw my mom. The last time I hung out with friends. My last day of work. The last night I took my kids to dinner. The last things I said to each of them. All of my lasts.

Now it was time for some firsts, starting with my first anniversary of survival.

30
SUNRISE

Friday, October 25

One year since the surgeries. One year since a little chest pain changed everything.

I came home to see balloons tied all around my front yard and porch and a decorated poster on my front door—a sweet, meaningful gesture from the friends who had supported me through so much. Apparently this day was my new birthday, and this year was the first celebration. I enjoyed watching the bright, colorful balloons float in the air on their long strings. It helped set a party mood.

The past couple days were nothing but a celebration of my life. Lunches, dinners, pedicures, massages, flowers, cards, gifts, phone calls, texts, emails—everyone got in touch to express how happy they were that I was still here. A whole year later, and the support never wavered. I could not believe how blessed I was.

I had dinner Thursday night with just me and my three amazing kids. We joked, we laughed, and we avoided talking about what we'd been doing a year earlier. (I actually suggested that we go to the hospital and hang out in the ICU waiting room all night. That joke didn't go over too well. McCall suggested dropping me off there by myself to spend five days waiting in agonizing suspense, since I'd slept through everything the first time.)

At the end of dinner, we shed tears and expressed our love for each other. The waiter took a picture of us. We all embraced just before leaving to go home, recognizing how blessed we were to share the gift of life together. We had a second chance.

The toughest day of the week was actually Tuesday. The last day I remembered before the surgeries was a Tuesday. Just a regular Tuesday, on which I woke to a regular day. Other than feeling more tired than usual, there was nothing remarkable about it. And then I died.

I cried as I thought of how I'd meandered through the ordinary day that could have been my last. No thought of what was coming. No knowledge of the horrors I was about to face. I felt scared for my past self in retrospect, terrified of what I now knew. Part of me wished again that it was just a bad dream. But it wasn't. It was reality. Like all those nights of torture sleeping on the couch, I had to endure it.

But every night leads to a sunrise.

It is now a few days after that anniversary. Tonight I decide to take down the balloons before they lose all of their helium. The sun sets as I walk into my front yard and begin untying them. I look up and decide to let them float away, up into the beautiful place where I have been and where I know I will return. They hover higher and higher, disappearing into the purple and amber sky as a fall breeze blows my hair away from my face. I take a deep breath.

I am alive.

I'm still not in perfect condition. At times I am very shaky. I fight through major fatigue and lethargy each day. My memory still has lapses, both short-term and long-term. My sense of direction is shot. Dr. Schorlemmer says I likely suffered some brain damage while I was frozen during the first surgery, and from the eighteen hours under anesthesia. Getting back all of my brain function may take years.

I still can't work out. We're waiting to see what happens next year. Hopefully I'll be able to start exercising again soon. I miss the muscles I spent so much time building. I want to start getting them back.

I still don't know exactly why this happened to me and not to someone else. Maybe I was prepared for it. I had the support, the loving family, the faith in my Father in Heaven, and the stubbornness to push my way through every challenge. I survived. I came through it. And now I can share my story to help others do the same.

I still have bad days. There are times I dream of waking up to the reality of a year ago, discovering that none of this was real. I still battle depression from time to time, and wish I had better explanations for all that's happened. I still have some bad nights where I wish I hadn't survived.

But there is always a sunrise.

Tonight I will make myself a cup of hot chocolate and drink it with my children. I will walk up the stairs and stand up during my shower. I will dress myself, crawl into my bed, and sleep curled up around my body pillow. I will remember the victories I've already obtained and pray for the strength to rise up and fight the next battle. I will feel my heart beat as I fall asleep and prepare for the next day. I will keep going.

I'm not at the beautiful place, but I know it's waiting for me. Until then,

I will strive to make this life the best it can be. I'll get there eventually. Tomorrow is just the next step.

EPILOGUE

Today

Every life has its ups and downs. Regardless of your circumstances, learn to be present in each season of your life. Life is meant to be lived, not just to exist.

If you are ill, remember that you are more than just a physical body. What can't be physically cured can often be emotionally healed. If you are sad, take charge of your mind and focus on the things that make you smile and laugh again. Find something worth living for and cling to it with all your might. Life is short. Don't allow anything to steal your joy. Celebrate the small victories, no matter how insignificant. Then look forward to the next victory and step out to achieve it.

There will be times when you have more questions than answers. Even in the darkest of those times, know that you are not alone. Be still. Listen to your heart. Allow yourself to hear your own still small voice. Believe in your truth. You have the power to create a valued, cherished, and celebrated life. You are something special. You have greatness within you.

Never take anything for granted, especially the magic of an ordinary day.

APPENDIX A
PHOTOS

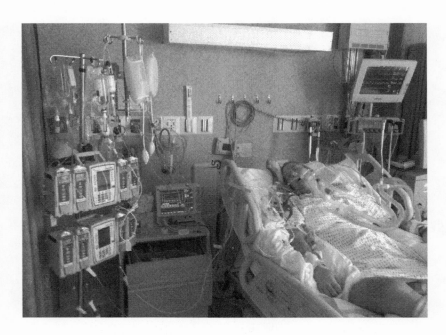

Sunday, October 28, 2012
My ICU room, with much of the equipment already removed

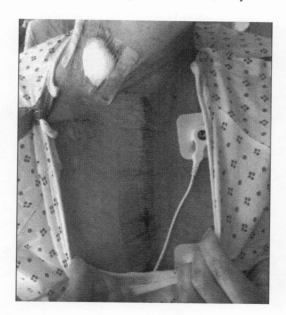

My incision, shortly after the surgeries

Hiking with Jace, summer of 2013

Family dinner, one year later

APPENDIX B
OTHER PERSPECTIVES

While preparing to write this book, I asked some of my family members and friends to write down their experiences during my surgeries and recovery. Those writings are collected here to provide additional perspectives on the entire ordeal.

By no means are these all of the people who deserve mention. There are countless other individuals who sacrificed their time and energy to support me. I am eternally grateful to all of them, and I hope you will draw insight and inspiration from the handful of viewpoints included here.

I am proud to honor these wonderful people who gave—and continue to give—me their incredible love and support throughout my healing process.

DR. SCHORLEMMER

When I first saw the CT scan images, I feared for her life. This type of aortic dissection is the worst injury that can happen to a human being. It is devastating. The majority of these patients don't survive.

What was worse for her than even other patients with the same condition was that the dissection had gone down to the root and was causing aortic valve leakage. Teri had the worst case of the worst case scenario.

But days later, she had pulled through. Teri was so blessed to have such amazing family and friends surrounding her and supporting her. The icing on the cake was to see her wake up and see her beautiful smile. No one should ever underestimate the gift of waking up each day.

She is a lucky and resilient woman, but what amazes me the most is how happy she is. It could be the worst day on the planet, and still she would manage to smile.

Sometimes the very worst things that happen to us end up being the best things. I think this is very true for Teri. She has an amazing story to share with the world.

MY MOM, MARY BETH NIEDERHAUSER

Early in the morning on October 24, 2012, my cell phone rang and I thought I was dreaming. I woke up and jumped out of bed, then ran to see who was calling so early in the morning. Before I could see who was calling on my cell, my home phone rang and I answered it.

On the other end of the phone was my son Wayne. I could not believe what he told me. Teri was in the hospital, having surgery for an emergency aortic dissection, and she might not make it. She would be in surgery for ten hours.

An aortic dissection? Well, what was that? I could not believe what he was telling me. Was I really hearing this right? Wayne tried to explain, but he was also extremely emotional and had a hard time talking. I hung up the phone and completely fell apart. Teri had been through so much already. I knelt down and said a prayer, pleading with the Lord to save her. She had to live for her three children.

I got in the car with tears in my eyes and wondered how I could drive to St. Mark's Hospital, about ninety miles south. I pulled myself together because I knew that I had to do it. I said another prayer and was on my way.

The next thing I remember, I was at the hospital. I could not remember driving down to Salt Lake City, and I couldn't believe I was at the hospital. To this day, I don't remember driving.

We were at the hospital for several hours before Dr. Schorlemmer came to talk to us and told us that she was not out of the woods yet. She could have a lot of problems because the operation took so long. She had a lack of blood flow that could affect her mind and several organs. He told us that two out of ten thousand make it through this operation. We were not to get our hopes up.

When we were able to go into the room to see her, it was very emotional for me. To see my beautiful daughter like that, my only daughter who had been through so much...it was almost unbearable.

The next day, she had another eight-hour emergency surgery to fix the blood flow to her kidneys, colon and liver. It broke my heart to see the devastation this surgery had taken on her.

While other people remarked how strong she was and said how she would be able to handle it, I was sad that she had to endure so much at all. How much more could her body take? Two *major* surgeries in less than two days? How much could her body rebound from?

She had a strong will to live for her three children. She maintained a positive attitude and fought to come out of this to live a normal life.

I am *so* proud of how she has handled all the trauma she has been through. Such an amazing daughter I have.

We have had a lot of help from Higher Powers in the journey of saving Teri's life. She is truly a miracle.

MY FRIEND REBECCA

It was six in the morning, and I was sound asleep. Rod, my husband, came into our room and said, "Honey, you have three missed calls from McCall."

"Why in the world would McCall be calling be at this time?" I was very concerned and went into "mom" mode. I quickly called her back. She was crying on the other end and trying to explain to me that her mom was in surgery for heart issues. I started asking a million questions, but then I realized that I just needed to listen and comfort her, even though inside I was dying.

She said Teri would be in surgery for several more hours. I told her I was on my way. I hadn't gotten the whole story from McCall, but I knew from the tone of her voice that it was serious.

At this time, my life was a little upside down. Teri had always been a source of strength to me. All the way to the hospital I pleaded with the Lord to not take her. Not now. Selfishly, I *needed* her to stay.

So much went through my mind as I drove the forty minutes to St. Mark's Hospital. How could Teri be having heart problems? She had just celebrated her fiftieth birthday by riding her bike fifty miles around Bear Lake. She had never been healthier. I just couldn't imagine what had happened.

As I arrived at the hospital, I put on my brave "mom" face. I knew I needed to be strong for McCall, Jace, and Dallin. As I got off the elevator, I was greeted with Benson hugs—big, teddy-bear-like hugs—that were filled with fear and disbelief. I looked every one of them in the eyes and told them with assurance, "Your momma is one strong lady, and she will not leave us. She will get through this." In my heart, I hoped what I promised was true.

After a few minutes, I walked over to Wayne, Teri's older brother. I asked him how he was, and then asked, "What is going on, Wayne? How is she, really?"

He said that just prior to surgery, Dr. Schorlemmer came to him and said, "This is very serious, and the chance of her coming out alive is very slim."

I looked at Wayne in horror. "Are you kidding me?"

"Rebecca, it will be a miracle."

Again in my heart I pleaded with my Heavenly Father, "Please don't take her now! There are too many people on this earth who need her beautiful, uplifting spirit. Please let her stay!"

I went over to McCall and asked her if she wanted to go for a little walk. I felt like I wanted to get her alone for a few minutes to just let her breathe. We walked the halls as she expressed to me what the past twelve hours had held. She is mature beyond her years and has always been there for her momma. She and my daughter Jennilyn were babies together, and I had watched this sweet girl grow up into a beautiful woman. A woman that needed her momma for many years to come. I hoped with all my heart that Teri would pull through this. She just had to.

When we got back to the waiting room, new visitors had arrived. I sat with Jace and Dallin, reassuring them that it would be okay. I felt like this would be a long journey, but she couldn't leave us.

After a few hours, Dr. Schorlemmer came out of surgery and asked us to gather in the family room. He wanted to tell us how things went. I immediately wanted to find a way to help, so I grabbed my yellow pad of paper and gathered with her family. As he spoke I took notes, since that's how I remember best. I asked lots of questions. But the bottom line was that the next forty-eight hours were critical. She wasn't out of the woods yet.

Once he left, we shared a family prayer together and pleaded for a miracle. We knew it was in the Lord's hands as to whether he needed her more in the spirit world than we needed her here. I hoped he knew how needed she was here! Many tears were shed, but still I was stoic. I needed to stay strong. It hadn't fully hit me yet that my best friend's life could be cut short.

Once the family was given the okay to go back to ICU to see her for a minute, I felt I needed to take my leave. I told McCall to keep me posted and that I would be close. They would all be in my prayers.

As I drove away from the hospital, the tears finally started to flow. *Please, oh please, Father, you can't take this dear woman from my life. I need her too much!*

I think it was that day that I realized how fragile life is, and how precious our relationships are to each other. I felt such a love for my dear friend and prayed that we could grow old together—laughing, crying, lifting, supporting, and building memories that would last forever.

I love you, Teri Benson. I am so grateful that the Lord decided that we needed you more on this earth. You are an incredible mother, woman, and friend. I treasure every day with you. I will always be here for you, just like you have always been here for me. You are amazing, and yes, we will grow old together.

MY OLDEST SON, DALLIN

On the morning of October 24, 2012, I was awakened by a call at five o'clock. From not getting much sleep the night prior, I could hardly open my eyes to realize that it was my sister, McCall. She was crying hysterically, and I could barely make out what she was saying to me. She was able to explain to me that Mom was having chest pains, and that she took her to the ER a few hours earlier. McCall said they had to rush her to St. Mark's Hospital, and that she would be undergoing an emergency open heart surgery momentarily.

I had never been more awake in my life after hearing her words. At that moment my whole paradigm shifted forever.

McCall said there wasn't much time before Mom went into surgery, and she quickly handed the phone to her. I immediately broke into tears upon hearing my mother's sweet voice. I quickly asked her what was going on and if she was ok. She sounded fatigued and didn't say much. All I could say was that I loved her and that I was praying for her.

I'll never forget what she said to me before I let her go. In a very tired and weak voice, she said, "Don't worry about me, Dallin. Everything will be ok."

It's hard to explain the emotions that went through me after hanging up the phone with her. Never in my life had I prayed with more sincere intent than I did that day.

That morning I had to attend two classes. As I got to school and sat down, I knew within the first ten minutes that I couldn't be there. I knew that my mom was going to be surgery for a long period of time, and I didn't want to sit at the hospital and anxiously wait for hours upon hours just yet. Instead I sat in my car in the school parking lot for about an hour, praying and praying for the surgeon to have the guidance he needed to save my mom's life.

I made my way to the hospital. On the way, I asked many family members and friends to pray for my mom that morning. I arrived at St. Mark's, and I had never been so overwhelmed with emotion and anxiety. As I was making my way up to where my family and friends were waiting, something definite came over me. I knew I had a duty and obligation to set an example for my younger brother and sister through this. I'm the oldest child, and it was on my shoulders to be the leader and assure them that everything was going to be okay. I quickly fought within myself, forcing out as much fear, worry, and uncertainty as I possibly could before walking into the waiting room.

When I arrived, I felt anxious to know all the answers about how this had happened to my mom. I remember trying to read on the Internet about her condition and how severe it really was. It probably wasn't the best idea, because I found out that most people don't live through this. In fact, most don't even make it to surgery, let alone survive the entire procedure and recovery. It was hard for me to deal with that knowledge because again, I knew I had to set the example and I couldn't show how scared I felt.

After waiting with family and friends for hours, we were finally told that they had finished the procedure. The nurse asked immediate family members to come to the back waiting room so the surgeon could speak to us.

It was a very small room, and we filled it up. I will never forget the excruciating anticipation. Everyone was so emotionally eager to hear from him. To make a longer story short, he told us that he did the best work he could possibly do in that operating room. He said there was quite a bit of damage to work through. As we all asked questions, he couldn't help but tell us how amazed he was with our mom. He had been a surgeon for over thirty years, and he spoke about her like she was one of a kind. You could tell that the procedure was unlike anything he had ever experienced.

We all just wanted to know if she was going to be ok. He was very sincere and honest in saying that, at that point, there was no telling, no straight answer. He explained that she had suffered major damage and that he was able to work through many complications. He was confident in saying that he did the best job he could do. It was not just about the surgery, but about the recovery as well. He said she was going to be moved to critical care in the ICU and that we would have to wait to see how her body was going to react to the catastrophe she had just been through.

It was very difficult to not get a straight answer that she was going to make it. After he left, I immediately asked to pray for her with our family and friends in that small room. I'll always remember the emotions and feelings that ran through me in that tiny waiting room after receiving the news from the surgeon.

Hours later, they had successfully moved her into the ICU, and they told us that her kids could come see her, one at a time. With all the trauma her poor body had experienced in the past fifteen hours, they told us she was going to be asleep for quite a while.

I remember going into the ICU and walking down the hall to her room. What a terrible feeling, having to see families crying after losing loved ones. I fought to have nothing but faith that my mom would be okay.

I approached her room and saw her from afar. It was like a slap in the face to see her in that condition. I couldn't even count the tubes and IVs that were connected to her body. It was extremely difficult to hold back the emotion I felt.

We left her to rest for the night. I hadn't eaten one thing all day, and I still wasn't hungry. That night I struggled, and I could tell my siblings were struggling too. That day seemed as if it were a whole week. It was a constant fight to keep my composure, but nothing was more important than keeping my brother and sister strong. The way that we came together was unlike anything I had ever experienced with them.

After a few days the surgeon felt another procedure on her heart was necessary to save her life. So, after another extensive surgery of six hours, she was back in the ICU on the ventilator to help her breathe. The next few days were the longest days of my life. Constant trips in and out of the hospital, not knowing what to expect each time I walked in the door. It almost felt like I was living there. To this day, I can't really explain the feeling I get when I drive past St. Mark's Hospital.

As we continued to visit and watch her closely, she battled to wake up and be fully conscious. It was the worst time of my life, watching her go through what she did. Every time she woke up, she was in complete misery. She wasn't herself at all, and it was truly difficult to watch. I felt sick inside seeing what all the drugs and anesthesia did to her body as she battled through this incredibly slow recovery. I got to the point where I didn't even go to visit her for a day. I couldn't stand to see her suffer.

When I looked into her eyes, I could see my real mom battling and fighting something ninety-nine percent of people won't experience in life. On the outside, she clearly wasn't herself, due to all the drugs and anesthesia. It was as if my mom was fighting for her life against all sorts of demons. It hurt me to watch her. I'm sincere when I say that I couldn't believe she was still alive at that point. As I continued to see my mom battle and suffer for days, I wondered deep down when it was going to pass. I wondered when good things were going to start to happen.

I hadn't slept in nights, and my eating habits decreased significantly. I was in a state of mind that I had never been in before and I believe I won't experience ever again.

As days passed, the worst time of my life transitioned into a miracle before my eyes. It was like in one day, everything I described earlier vanished. My mom finally woke up, and for the first time in nearly a week I saw her REAL, beautiful smile. I never anticipated her showing the amazing signs of progress that she suddenly did. It was the greatest gift to see her talking, smiling, and being herself.

I cannot even fathom going through what she experienced. With all the positive progress she was making, ten days after her life-threatening heart condition, the doctors cleared her to move into a normal hospital room. You can only imagine how badly she wanted to be back in the comfort of her own home.

Just two days after that, they gave us the big news. She was finally cleared to return home! What a feeling it was for me and my siblings to take our mom back home. I felt at peace for the first time in two weeks.

What I described here doesn't do the least bit of justice of what the actual experience was like, but I tried to do my best in reiterating it. What I saw over those twelve days will stay with me for the rest of my life. God is great, and I was able to witness and be a part of a miracle. It was a pivotal experience of personal growth for me to go through that.

I'll never be able to give enough thanks to all of our family members and friends who prayed for her and supported her though this. What a blessing to have such wonderful people in our lives.

I love you, Teri Lyn Benson, and I am forever grateful to be your son. You taught me that miracles can happen if you fight and never give up. You were kept here on earth for many reasons. I look forward to seeing you live happily and abundantly in this life.

MY FRIEND ALBA MCGOWAN

I remember struggling at times with the concept of faith. Wondering why seemingly bad things happen to good people. This is what came to mind when I first received the upsetting news that my dear and beautiful friend Teri was in the hospital. I was told that she was in extremely critical condition and that her chances of survival were slim.

Upon hearing this, I started to shake uncontrollably. I became more upset as I learned how dire the situation was. But then I remembered how many times Teri had faced obstacles in her life, and how many times she overcame them with her chin up and a big smile on her face. I really believed that if anybody could come out of this all right, it was Teri. Time and time again, through every challenge in her life, she taught me strength, faith, and grace. I made the conscious and deliberate decision to believe that she would be okay. After all, this was Teri.

I wanted to be near her. I wanted to see her and reassure her. I knew she was in good hands, but I worried about her children, her loved ones. She was in the critical care unit, and only her closest family members were allowed to visit. Teri's daughter McCall was so sweet, giving us updates on her mother's condition whenever she could. Many of Teri's friends and family came to the hospital every day to provide support, encouragement and comfort to her children. They would sit out in the waiting room for hours, and they would go back home without seeing Teri. Unfortunately her condition was just too critical for her to receive visitors.

Then, on a Sunday morning, I finally got the green light from McCall to meet her at the hospital so that she could try to let me in to see Teri.

I arrived at the hospital early, so McCall was still en route. I took the elevator and found the Do Not Enter sign posted on the automatic double-doors of the critical care unit. There were no people around, and I was so anxious to go in. I paced around for a while and then said a silent prayer.

Then, as if on cue, the double doors suddenly opened. I just walked right in, desperate to find Teri's room.

I ran into a couple of nurses in the hallway and asked them where Teri was. They kindly pointed me in the right direction, seeming to assume I was a close family member of hers, even though we look nothing alike. I walked into the room alone. It was just Teri and I in there, her eyes closed and her body hooked up to many machines, one of which was actually breathing for her. She appeared so vulnerable.

I experienced many emotions when I saw her. I felt concerned and helpless, and happy at the same time to finally see her. Most of all, I was hopeful that it wouldn't be the last time I saw her.

After I watched her for a couple of minutes, the same nurses that directed me to Teri's room walked in with some equipment and moved to one side of her bed so they could work on her. I asked them if they thought Teri could hear someone talking to her. One of them said they didn't know. I then asked if it would be okay if I said a few words while they worked on her. To my relief, they answered yes.

Finally faced with the opportunity to speak to her, I wondered what I would want to hear the most if I was the one lying there instead. I walked closer to the edge of her bed and put my hand on the small area of her arm that wasn't covered in tape, electrodes, or IVs. I put my face next to hers and said softly, "Hi Teri, this is Alba."

In response, she opened her eyes. Blinking and unfocused, they began to move around as she looked for me. The nurses said she couldn't turn her head because of the breathing machine. I continued speaking, and I told Teri that she didn't have to worry about anything. I told her that she would be okay, that her children were well taken care of, that there was such an outpouring of love and support from her family and friends, and that she was not alone. I could tell she understood because her eyes grew watery and she smiled for me, despite the breathing tube running through her mouth. She was still smiling throughout everything.

One of the nurses said I should stop talking to her because her blood pressure was starting to increase. So I told her I loved her, kissed her forehead, and left.

In the following days, Teri made an astonishing recovery and was able to leave the hospital a lot sooner than her doctors and the rest of us expected. Teri pulled through and made the meaning of faith tangible for me. She continues to be a great example of strength and perseverance to all of us who are fortunate enough to know her.

MY YOUNGER BROTHER,
DAVID NIEDERHAUSER

Back on October 24, 2012, I got a call early in the morning from my brother, Wayne. I cannot remember the time, but it woke me up, and my alarm was set for five thirty. When you get a call from family between eleven p.m. and seven a.m., it can't be good news.

When I rolled over and saw Wayne's name on my phone, I first thought something had happened to Mom. He said Teri was at the hospital to have emergency heart surgery. He mentioned an aortic dissection. He explained a little about what it was and said it was serious, but should be okay.

The weather was bad in Utah, and I asked Wayne if Mom was aware of what was going on. He said she was aware, but because of the bad weather and snowy roads he had told her not to drive to Salt Lake. I told him I would take care of a few things at work and drive out to the city from California. He said to wait until we had more info when she got out of surgery.

After the phone call, I got on my computer to look up aortic dissections. I figured it was another name for a type of heart attack, and from people I knew who'd had heart attacks, early medical attention was the key to a successful treatment. I figured Teri was in the hospital, so all would be well, until I found "aortic dissection" on the Internet.

The one statistic I looked at said that eighty percent of patients do not make it through this. My thoughts went back ten years ago to when we found out my dad had pancreatic cancer. I remembered thinking about surgery and chemo therapy and assuming all would be well until I looked up pancreatic cancer. After looking it up on the Internet, I quickly realized that he would *not* be okay. A year later he passed away.

After I looked up aortic dissections, Wayne called me back and said that he had talked to the doctor, and things were NOT okay. He said Mom was getting ready to drive down. He said for me not to rush out right now, but to wait until after the surgery. I could tell in his voice that it did not look good. I remember thinking that the fact she was still alive at this point may be a good start.

That morning I drove to my office and let everyone know what was going on. I tried to get my work in order to leave for a few days. Later that afternoon, Wayne called and said Teri was out of surgery and in recovery. When I was reading about aortic dissections on the Internet, one article stated that even if the patient makes it through surgery, that thirty percent do not make it through recovery and that there was only a sixty percent chance to make it ten years. The statistics were not in Teri's favor.

My thoughts were with Teri's kids and what they must be going through. A few months earlier, my family and I visited Utah and spent some time with Teri. She was looking great. She was in excellent shape and seemed very happy. It was good to see her like that. How would she be feeling now?

That next day, my family and I climbed in the car and headed for Salt Lake. We spent the night in St. George, getting updates from Mom and Wayne on the way there. Wayne called again and said that Teri would be going into surgery again because her organs were not getting the blood they need to continue working. She was in surgery while we were heading to Salt Lake from St. George.

I was very nervous about going to see Teri. I did not want to see her in that condition. We dropped off the kids at Wayne's house and waited until we could see her in the ICU. We got to the hospital, and Wayne and I went in to see her and to give her a blessing. She was groggy and definitely thirsty. All she wanted was a drink of water, and she thought she was going to die unless she had water immediately. I felt so bad for her at that time, thinking of what she had gone through.

We asked her if we could give her a blessing, and she said we could, but only if we gave her some water. The nurse gave her a swab with some water on it, wiped it on her lips, and let her suck on it. It did not help her thirst. We can laugh about that now and it has become a family joke, but at the time, it was heartbreaking. Teri told the nurse in front of McCall, Wayne, and I that if she could not get water now, that she wanted to die. I remember tearing up when she said that. I had to keep telling myself that she was highly medicated and didn't know what she was saying.

Wayne and I proceeded to give her a blessing, and I had a strong feeling as we were giving the blessing that she was going to live. I knew things were not good and that it was going to take some time, but knew she would be able to return home with her family.

My family spent a few more days in Salt Lake City, and my wife and I visited Teri daily while we were there. Each time we were there, I cried and felt so bad for her and her situation. I kept asking how and why this could happen.

I had always heard that bad things happening to good people could be learning and growth opportunities. At the time I wondered what Teri and her family, along with us, would learn from this situation.

I prayed—and continue to pray—for Teri and her family, that they would all heal and recover and find the silver lining that is hidden somewhere within the situation. For me, since this happened, I have tried to spend special moments with my wife and kids together and individually, and to give them my full attention. Work and daily routines will always be there, but the time we spend with family will always be remembered. I also increased my life insurance, knowing that anything can happen at any time.

My family and I reluctantly had to leave on Monday afternoon to get the kids back to school and me back to work. During the trip, I was only able to see Teri in the ICU in a medicated state, but I was so thankful for the work that all the medical staff did to help her get through this. My wife and I frequently reflect back on that time, and we still cannot believe Teri went through that whole ordeal. Miracles do happen.

MY FRIEND LAURA STEVENS

As I got off the elevator and glanced over at Teri's family and friends, I knew in a heartbeat that this wasn't the news any of us wanted to hear. Dr. Schorlemmer was talking quietly as I approached, and McCall stood up and motioned for me to come over. In that moment, a flood of thoughts rushed over me. If I stayed right here in the hallway, I didn't have to deal with life and death. I could keep Teri alive in my mind, just as I saw her forty-eight hours ago—bounding off to the gym in her hot pink T-shirt, black shorts, and her worn-out running shoes. She tossed some snarky statement and a smile at me as she left. I called after her, "Have fun, and see you in the morning!" From the hushed tones I now heard among her family members, I hoped beyond all hope that those were not the last words I ever spoke to my dear friend.

I walked over and joined the group banded together because of one woman fighting for her life. As I looked into their faces, I saw exhaustion, confusion, and blank stares. A few questions were asked of the surgeon, and I heard the words "dialysis," "colostomy bag," and "the next twenty-four hours are crucial." So much information in such a short time. I could see from their blank faces they were battle weary.

We had been fighting against all odds for over seventy-two hours, willing our mother, daughter, sister, and friend to live. I believe we all were calling in favors from God and making whatever promises needed to turn the tide in this fight for her life.

The surgeon left and the silence weighed heavily upon our group. McCall looked over at me and offered a smile. She continued to rally Team Teri. She was a real trooper, processing all this information and sharing it with so many, all of whom continued to send thoughts and prayers on Teri's behalf.

I put my arm around McCall, and a thought came to mind: *Bide your time*

169

and hold out hope.

Jace sat across from McCall, looking exhausted. He didn't say much, but his eyes reflected the pain he was feeling. And yet, he continued to smile. It was contagious, and I smiled back, grateful for the encouragement after hearing such devastating news about his mom. I appreciated the quiet strength he offered. I needed to remember to tell Teri about her amazing children pushing on against these insurmountable odds. She would be so proud. She had taught them well.

Then it dawned on me to find some photos of Teri and put them in her room so that those taking care of her would know why this amazing woman was so precious to us. And then we waited. The phrase "let go and let God" came to mind, which is so very hard to do when the life of someone so dear hangs in the balance.

Several weeks went by as I watched my dear friend continue on this healing path. I kept thinking about a quote Teri shared with me: "When your life gets destroyed, build a new one, and build it better." Step by step, I realized that she was doing exactly that.

On a cold February afternoon, I slipped away on my lunch hour for a visit. We sat by the fire and talked about how great it would be when she reached that wellness mark of being able to experience an ordinary day. You don't realize how amazing it is to have an ordinary day until it is out of your reach.

We talked about what she would like to do, and we paused, as we both knew part of her ideal ordinary day would be to take her bike out on one of her fifty-mile treks. I stopped, not wanting to bring up a painful reminder of what she couldn't do, only to have her tell me about all the handsome guys she met at cardiac rehab, wearing heart monitors and opening up a whole new dating pool! We both laughed, realizing that her ordinary day now may not look the same as it once did, but that that didn't make it any less spectacular.

Thank you, my dear, brave friend, for your strength and these beautiful life lessons you have taught me.

MY OLDER BROTHER, WAYNE NIEDERHAUSER

Could I hear a phone ringing? I thought I was dreaming. It was five thirty in the morning! Should I answer? Who could be calling? "Don't bother me now, I am sleeping."

Wait, it was my sister. What would she be calling about? I answered hesitantly. "Hello?"

"Uncle Wayne!" I heard a sobbing voice on the other end of the line. "This is McCall. We're at Lone Peak Hospital. Mom has been having chest pains. The tests are not good. She needs to go to St. Mark's Hospital for emergency surgery. Can you come and give her a blessing?"

These weren't the exact words that McCall and I exchanged over the phone early that morning on October 24, 2012, but the content is the same. Teri is my only sister. We grew up together and were very close. She was in trouble. How much trouble, I knew not. I knew it was serious; McCall was very disturbed.

"Can you come and give her a blessing?" McCall asked.

"Yes, of course," was my response.

Teri was just leaving Lone Peak Hospital in an ambulance. I told McCall that I would meet them there as quickly as I could.

I was barely awake, so I paused to gather my thoughts. Who could I ask to go with me to assist in the blessing?

Ethan, of course, was the immediate response in my mind. One floor below in our basement, a young man lay sound asleep. My nineteen-year-old son was less than three weeks from going on his LDS mission to Wisconsin. "He was recently ordained as an elder," I thought to myself. This would be a good way for him to learn about giving blessings, one of the many priesthood duties of an elder. More importantly, his aunt had an urgent, serious need. Faith was calling us.

Teri and McCall believed in priesthood blessings. They had experienced and seen firsthand the results of miracles. Teri's life had been saved at least a couple times before because of faith in the power of the priesthood.

Waking Ethan had never been easy. It takes a bomb to blow him out of bed. Calling to him in the night, I repeated his name. Finally, I heard a grunt of sorts. "Teri needs a blessing," I told him. "She is going in for emergency heart surgery. We need to go now."

Ethan threw back the covers and jumped out of bed like a rocket. I couldn't believe someone could do that without all the blood rushing out of their head.

We both dressed in our Sunday best. Working as a servant of God requires one to look the part, since we would be representing Him. Before we left, we knelt in prayer together in my home office. We asked the Father to spare our sister and aunt and to give us the worthiness and ability to be heavenly spokesmen in granting a blessing and miracle for Teri. We still did not know the seriousness of her situation. I made sure that we didn't forget the consecrated anointing oil.

The drive to St. Mark's Hospital was mostly reflective, but I remember rehearsing for Ethan the steps to giving a priesthood blessing. The drive was not unfamiliar to me. Four of my five children, including Ethan, had been born in that hospital, though several years before. In that time, the hospital had made some fairly significant changes to the facilities. It took some navigating to figure out where to go once we arrived at the hospital.

Teri was in the ICU, getting prepared for surgery. Ethan and I walked into her room. McCall was there, and she continued to be there through the entire process as Teri's rock of support. There were nurses coming and going in preparation for the operation.

Teri looked good, but I could tell that she was worried. She tried to minimize the seriousness of the situation and attempted to keep things on the light side. This was pretty typical for my sister. I followed along, trying to avoid any serious conversation, but to no avail. This *was* serious. This was open heart surgery. I had never heard of an aortic dissection. "Can the wall of the aorta really separate?" I wondered to myself. It seemed like a dream.

The surgeon informed us about the procedure. I just remember him talking about things like freezing her body and having her blood bypass the heart through a machine, and saying that she would be in surgery for as much as seven to eight hours. Thoughts kept running through my mind: How could someone survive that kind of trauma? What about the surgeon, Doctor Schorlemmer? Was he competent? Did he know what he was doing? I heard comment after comment from hospital staff that he was one of the best and that Teri was in the best possible hands.

The doctor took me aside into the hallway and confidentially told me that her situation wasn't good. "Teri would be lucky to survive," he said. He gave her a fifty/fifty chance, but he told me after the surgery that it was really a twenty percent chance. He said that someone in the family should know the gravity of the situation without diminishing the hope of other family members.

Ethan and I gave Teri the requested blessing. He did the anointing and I sealed the anointing. I don't remember the details of the words that were spoken on her behalf, but I do remember saying that God miraculously preserves our lives at times in order to give us every opportunity to accept His will. It is human nature to ignore our Heavenly Father until we desperately need help. He must grow weary of our temporary allegiances and our broken promises. We blessed Teri to be healed and realized that God expected her to draw near to Him and to fulfill sacred covenants made with Him throughout her life. This would be another chance.

After this tear-filled experience, kisses and love were exchanged, and Teri was wheeled out to surgery. As I watched her disappear out of sight, I wondered if we would see her again in mortality, but I had faith in the Priesthood and the power of the blessing.

There was little we could do while she was in surgery, so I took Ethan home and went to work for a couple of hours. I returned to the hospital later in the morning to offer support to Dallin, Jace, and McCall while they waited. My mother had come to offer her support. This was very traumatic for her as well. There were many tears shed and prayers offered.

Teri has always had a natural ability to connect with people in a profound way. Instantly, new friends become devoted soul mates. Through the day of surgery and the many months that followed, these friends offered endless support and help. Unexpectedly for Teri, she needed all the support she could get to recover from such an invasive operation.

Finally, the operation was over. We had all fretted over her and pled with heaven on her behalf. Doctor Schorlemmer briefed us on the results. "She was a lucky lady," he said. The operation had gone well, but was cut short in order to avoid the high risks of brain damage involved with putting her on ice and lowering her body temperature. (Whenever Teri does something deficient now, we just blame it on the ice.) The Doctor told us that he could finish the necessary procedures later through the femoral artery once she had some time heal. He also told us that we could see her shortly, but that we would need to limit our numbers and time in order to avoid agitating her. The aorta was fragile, and it was best to avoid anything that would affect the delicate process of healing.

One of the best, yet most heart-wrenching comedies I have ever seen was Teri's recovery from the surgery. She was obviously not herself, but she exhibited some of her stubbornness. She couldn't have any water for some time, but her throat was extremely dry. Teri wanted water at all costs. It made me sad, yet it was funny in retrospect. We wanted to give another blessing, but she wouldn't let us. Her first and only condition was getting water.

Much to her chagrin, recovery was slow, and then she had the follow-up surgery that set her back. The months afterward were tough for her. I think she experienced every emotion. At times, it was downright depressing. There was constant fatigue, short periods of time when she felt good, and then she would overdo herself to the point of setback. But Teri is hard to keep down. She is a goer and a doer.

Through it all I knew she had hope. It was represented by her bike. Many months before her operation, Teri had started road cycling, and she loved the newfound sport. She had purchased a bike and enjoyed getting out on the road. We had talked several times about cycling together, but sadly had never hooked up for a ride.

She kept her bike in the living room of her home. For months after the surgery, it remained there. I wondered why she didn't put it away, because it was obvious that it would be months before she could ride. In fact, there was talk that she might never be able to get on the bike again. I think she left it there in the living room to give her hope and to remind herself of the life she still wanted to live. I believe that it helped in her recovery. I can still see in my mind that bike leaning against the north wall.

Through it all, there is one thing we never forget. Teri is a miracle. She had a very competent surgeon, but it was also God who guided the doctor's skillful hands that day, and He who healed Teri's body. Teri is preserved because God has granted her an extension. He has an errand for her. I hope she discovers that mission.

I love her with all my heart.

MY SON JACE

Just like any ordinary night, I was hanging out by the fire, getting cozy, when my mom and sister walked downstairs at a late hour. I asked, "What's up?"

McCall said, "Mom isn't feeling well, and she has a pain in her chest."

"Should I come with you guys?"

Mom answered, "No, no, I'll be fine. Just go to bed."

So I waited and waited. Then McCall called me with news that immediately put me at the lowest of lows. My heart dropped to my stomach. It had immediately became the worst news I had every received.

My mom is everything to me, so I didn't know what to think. Just hearing the words "open heart surgery" scared me so much. With my mind racing a million miles an hour, all I could do was wait and wait to see how she was doing after the first long surgery. It didn't feel real because of the intense, scared feelings—something I had never felt, and hope to never feel again. Hours and hours later, my mom's condition was still uncertain, as she has been in surgery for almost ten hours. I still don't even want to think about these memories to this day.

My feelings were unexplainable. The help and love and prayers from all of our friends and family were amazing. I had never felt more loved than this time in our lives. Our friends and family helped us tremendously, and we wouldn't have been able to make it without them.

After grueling days of no appetite for food, music, or even the will to live, my mom's condition was still uncertain. But upon a few blessings, prayers, and miracles, my mom showed signs of improvement, and the doctor also showed positivity about her overall condition.

After all we had been through, it was such a relief to go into Mom's hospital room and see that she was alert. Over time in the hospital, things became better, and the time came for her to come home. That was another

175

story of its own, which you know from the rest of this book.

My mom is the strongest woman I know and has gone through many life-threatening trials—things most people never have to endure in a whole lifetime. She represents strength, love, and perseverance. She is my everything, and I am so glad to call her my mom.

I love you, Mom.

MY FRIEND LINDSI

I received a text from a mutual friend that Teri was having heart surgery. It may sound backwards, but my first reaction was irritation. Teri had been known to have surgeries, disasters, and family emergencies and not tell anyone about them. Teri hates to inconvenience anyone, and would offer her standard "I'm fiiiiiiine" in reply to offers of help.

My irritation quickly turned to fear as I continued to read the text filling in the lost details. I had just talked to Teri the night before. We were going to exercise together, but she had tickets to Thriller. Teri and I had exercised together for over seven years. I had seen her strengthen both her physical exterior as well as her emotional interior. I had *no* idea how critical her preparation for this moment would become.

McCall answered my call and filled me in. By this time, Teri was already in surgery. I made arrangements to visit when they expected her to be out. McCall vented about a few family dynamics and told me that she was now the signer for Teri. She would be calling the shots. At the young age of twenty, she was doing what I pray I never have to do for my loved ones. At that point, I felt like McCall chalked this experience up to Teri using one her depleting nine lives. I don't think anyone was prepared for what was about to unfold.

When I arrived at the hospital, Teri was out of surgery and in the critical care unit. McCall and I walked and talked. She filled me in on how the boys were coping. Dallin was straight-faced, and Jace was a mess. McCall then said that we should go back to see Teri. I was surprised and, to be honest, completely caught off guard. My intention for this visit was to just show support.

I excused myself to the bathroom in hopes of preparing myself emotionally. The last time I was in adult critical care was over a decade ago, when my grandmother was dying. I tried to trick myself using mental imagery. I wanted to expect the worse, and so that was what I envisioned. I pictured Teri, half dead and fighting for existence. I started to tear up with the frail idea of mortality, especially as it concerned my dearest Teri.

I broke down for about five seconds and then gave myself an figurative slap across the chops. I told myself that I would not cry. I would keep it together for Teri. She didn't need a pity party. I was going to help make her happy, even for a moment. That was all I wanted.

McCall and I waited to be buzzed in, which felt like an eternity. The doors separated, and the smell of death punched me in the face. As we made our way back to Teri's room, I looked in every other patient's room in the hope that it would diminish the shock when I finally reached Teri.

When I stepped into the room, I felt like I had stepped into a cold shower. Teri looked like a cartoon, as if someone had colored her skin grey. McCall announced in a clear voice that I had come to see her. I stepped closer to her bed, and she painfully lifted her heavy eyes. I smiled and held her hand.

Teri looked at her body and then into my eyes. She quietly said, "Sorry."

Up until that point, my eyes had seen the pain and suffering, but I'd held it together. When Teri said "sorry," my spirit broke. I didn't know what to say. I froze.

A nurse walked in and explained to McCall that Teri's heart rate was rising and that it was a good idea to hold off on any more visitors. I mustered up enough words to tell Teri that I loved her and that I would see her soon. McCall and I walked out the same, long, death-filled corridor we'd entered through. I had failed miserably. The confidence and faith I had brought into the hospital had been ripped apart by fear.

It is weird how perspective changes. When Teri and I first became friends, it was a comfortable place. Our friendship consisted of workouts, birthday lunches, shopping, laughs, and one-liners. As our lives progressed, the surface friendship was eliminated, and instead a raw friendship formed. When I say raw, I mean emotional—fighting, pleading mercy, and relentless struggles. These are not the things that you grab a cup of coffee over. These moments are ones you wished you didn't even have, let alone share with someone else.

I had seen Teri crawl out of emotional hell more times than I could count. I really felt like she had become the female Job. Rocky marriage, heart attack, cancer, going back to work, serious illness with her children, divorce, losing her house, moving—these were just surface descriptions. The emotional wrestling she withstood would have done me in. You literally had to push your way past her reflex of insisting that life was fine. (Never take someone's word when they say they are "fine," especially Teri. She's a liar.) She tried to hold the weight on her shoulders while discouraging *anyone* from watching while she did it.

Looking at Teri lying in her bed, swollen, bruised, sprawled out as if she were already dead, I couldn't recall any of her previous Goliath-like strength. It was like getting hit over the head. I fell dumb. She was vulnerable, and I could do nothing to help. I was terrified. My faith had been rocked.

I watched family and friends react to her pain in a range of emotion. I saw sheer panic, defeat, and faith.

Faith. It's a simple idea, but the challenge is the application. How can you move forward in faith when fear is breathing down your neck? I forced myself to remain positive.

I did find an answer amidst the pain. The adversities Teri had faced before this moment were meant to prepare her to overcome, not to beat her down into submission. She had the fight in her, and she needed positivity, as we all do. When life is difficult, we don't need to be reminded of it. We need someone in our corner.

On the outside, it may seem like we were serving Teri, but it's the complete opposite. Teri is the servant to us all. I can think of no other human being who has persevered like Teri. She has a greater calling, and this experience will help her answer that call.

MY FRIEND WENDI

Just thinking of that day gives me a knot in my stomach. I woke up to a text from McCall that said Teri had been taken in for emergency heart surgery. What the crap? Did I read that right? My heart sank. Not Teri. She had been through so much already.

"Wait," I thought. "What did she say? It was her heart?" In my mind, Teri was a pillar of health. Who spent more time exercising than she did?

I called McCall and got no answer. That only scared me more. I dressed and drove to St. Mark's Hospital. As I drove, I prayed and pleaded with God.

My first thought was of the kids. So many emotions ran through my head. My sister had lost her husband at a young age to heart problems, so I knew firsthand how hard such an ordeal could be on a family. But I knew Teri was a fighter. She would do everything she could on her end to pull through this. She would fight.

I guess that sounds a bit silly, considering that it was more or less out of her hands. But I couldn't think anything other than: *She. Will. Pull. Through.*

I arrived at the hospital to find McCall, Jace, Dallin, Teri's mother, and her older brother waiting. The looks on their faces broke my heart. The kids all gave me hugs and thanked me for coming. McCall hugged me and then broke down crying.

Oh, these poor kids! What could I say to them? They knew what a trooper their mom was, but still nothing I could say would ease their pain at that moment. I felt like they were in shock, not believing the reality of what was happening.

The waiting continued. I had brought snacks and drinks, and I did my best to get everyone to eat something. McCall settled on a Diet Coke. The poor girl was sick to her stomach with grief.

My husband, Greg, called to check in. He wanted to know which doctor

180

was performing the surgery and what exactly was going on. My brother-in-law is a heart surgeon in the Salt Lake Valley area, so my husband wanted to call him to learn more about this type of surgery and what exactly an aortic dissection was.

More waiting. We shared fun Teri stories and did our best to stay positive. McCall shared the E.T. phone home video, and we laughed.

She. Will. Pull. Through.

My husband called back. He told me to step away from the family. Once again my heart sank. He informed me that though my brother-in-law knew only the basic information that I had relayed about Teri, he knew enough about this type of condition to say that the news bad. An aortic dissection was not a condition that a lot of people walked away from. If it was as severe as I had described, Teri's outlook was not good. However, she was in excellent hands. Dr. Schorlemmer was a highly recommended surgeon.

Oh, what should I say to the kids? I prayed again and went back to the waiting room. I said nothing, though I relayed the part about Dr. Schorlemmer being the doctor to have if someone had to go through such a thing.

Teri's friend Rebecca showed up. She brought a notepad and was ready to get some answers. We all felt grateful that someone actually thought to write down what the doctor and nurses were telling us.

A nurse gave us a brief update. Not many answers, but she remained confident. We continued to hope.

Finally, after what felt like an eternity, the nurse came to collect the family and a couple of close friends. We were ushered into a small room to wait for the results. My stomach felt sick.

Dr. Schorlemmer came in with the news. He explained that Teri had so much damage that it was a miracle that she had made it through the surgeries. "She has gone a thousand miles, but has a million more to go."

It was so emotional, just knowing that she had pulled through. It was hard to think about what obstacles Teri would have to overcome in the future. Right then we were just so grateful that our prayers had been answered.

She. Pulled. Through.

Being Teri's "sister," I was let into the ICU to see her. Oh, my dear friend! She looked like she had been hit by a train. But she smiled at me as I held her hand.

If anyone could make a full recovery, it was Teri Benson.

AUNT JANICE

Teri Niederhauser came into my life for a reason. She became Teri Benson after marrying my nephew and will forever be a most cherished part of my life. Teri once gave me a book about opening your heart to others, and I know our relationship was based on this principle. I feel this book was a gesture of support and care from Teri, and it guided me to a place of always having an open heart for her.

In life's chain of events, nothing is accidental. Everything happens according to an inner need, and indeed, I needed Teri in my life. She married into my family; therefore, we are not blood relatives. That did not keep us from becoming the best of friends. Kurt Langner said, "Love is a gift. You can't buy it, you can't find it. Someone has to give it to you."

Teri and I have been through many experiences together—some happy and gratifying, some sad and challenging. But none more stressful than the call I received on October 24 from McCall, telling me her mom was in the hospital with heart problems. At that time McCall didn't know the severity of the situation, and I assumed it was probably something similar to the slight heart attack she'd had previously. McCall said she would be in surgery for quite some time, so I should not come to the hospital yet. I work very close to the hospital, so I said I would go into work and come to see her after the surgery.

I made it to about three o'clock and then could wait no longer. When I got to the hospital, the news awaiting me was horrifying. The family gathered in a room for a prayer and the doctor's arrival. The surgery was finished, and he was coming in to explain how it went. Aortic dissection? What was that? I had never heard of it, but at that point I knew it was not a good problem to have. Prayers and positive vibes began to process in my brain. No way were we going to lose our Teri.

The next few weeks, my feelings were up and down. One minute I had hope, and then the next she was going back into another serious surgery, and I felt despair. Then hope again, and on and on. But I told Teri later that I had the strongest feeling from the beginning that she would not leave us.

Sitting in the hospital day after day, crying, loving the children, crying, sharing experiences with family and friends, crying. I thought I would focus on the positive things that happened during that time. I have to say that what I witnessed from Teri's friends was unbelievable. The acts of kindness that filled that hospital and her home were undoubtedly the acts of angels. Her friends kicked in and had everything taken care of in no time—meals for the children, people to clean her home, bringing food to the children and family at the hospital. The list goes on and on. I couldn't begin to tell all the things they did for her and her family.

I couldn't believe what I witnessed. The compassionate service they gave to Teri and her family was so instinctive and natural for them. These were people she worked with, exercised with, had known for quite some time where she lived, etc. I got to know several of these people while sitting in the hospital, and they are truly God's angels. These people exemplified that kindness and service are at the root of all that is good. Kindness permeates everything it contacts. They were kind people! I am so grateful for the opportunity to know them, even though it was not under the most favorable circumstances. How fortunate Teri is to have them in her life.

Gratitude is the feeling I experience when I think of Teri—gratitude for her being in my life. Gratitude for the blessings she has brought me. A French proverb by Jean Baptiste Massieu says that "gratitude is the heart's memory," and Teri is forever in my heart. I could not imagine my life without her, and I am grateful that I did not have to. It was not her time. God knew that we needed her.

I hope that what I have written in some way expresses the unconditional love I have for Teri. Love is such an exceptional word. It helps us enjoy our world, makes us better people, and gives us greater friendships. Teri is that greater friendship in my life—one who knows how I feel, listens to how I think, and understands me. I hope I am that same kind of friend for her. To be true friends, you must be sure of one another, and I think we feel safe and know that we can trust each other implicitly.

Teri, I will cherish you forever, and I love you so much!

MY DAUGHTER, MCCALL

When your mom is your best friend, your rock, the only dependable person in your life, almost losing her is unbearable. Life would no longer have an appeal to it. Having my mom live is the reason I'm still here today.

It was a regular night. I was in bed watching Netflix when my mom knocked at my door. She told me she had a tiny, stinging pain in her chest and asked if I would take her to the ER. Anyone who knows my mom knows she is not one to cry wolf, so I knew this was serious. I got up and changed my clothes, and five minutes later we were on our way to the hospital. All I could think of was the need to hurry. I couldn't drive fast enough. My mom was squeezing the sides of her armrests. She was in pain. *Hurry up, McCall,* I thought. *Hurry.*

When we got to the ER, my mom told the nurses it probably wasn't a big deal. Ha. We went back into a room and they ran some tests, but they couldn't figure it out. In the beginning, my mom was being her usual self and making some jokes about being at the ER in the middle of the night. Then it turned into tears streaming down her face. That's when I got a terrible feeling that this was serious. My mom was in pain. Something wasn't right. She needed help, *now.*

After what felt like hours, they took her to get an MRI of her chest. When she came back, we waited for the doctors to check it out. Finally her doctor came back in. He told us she was having something called an aortic dissection. A what? What's that? He was very calm and vague, and he said they were going to get her all fixed up. An ambulance was coming to take her to St. Mark's right now. My mom looked confused and asked if they had to cut her open, and I remember the doctor's response word for word: "Yes, you're going in to have emergency open heart surgery."

What? *Keep it together McCall. Stay calm. It will be okay. Be strong and keep your mom calm.* That was all I could think. I had never seen my mom so scared in her life.

The doctor left us alone for a minute, and we talked about what to do. We needed to call my uncle and brothers first. My mind raced. I couldn't think straight.

Finally the ambulance arrived, and we took off for St. Mark's. My uncle was waiting there for us, and we headed up to the critical care unit where they had taken my mom.

When we got to her room, my mom was laying in the hospital bed with what seemed like a million doctors and nurses around her, checking this, looking at that, poking her with needles here, putting IVs in there. It was all happening so fast that it didn't seem real.

What is happening? Is this a nightmare? What is happening to my mom? This can't be real. I can't do this. I can't handle this. I need my mom!

I looked over, trying to see the expression on my mom's face. It was blank, with tears just streaming down the sides of her face.

Her surgeon came in, and the room went silent. He went over the surgery with us and told my mom there was a twenty percent chance he could do this, but that he would do the best he could. The terms and extent of everything he said was so extreme that I knew my mom wouldn't be coming out of this. This was it.

I stood in the corner of her room, bawling. I couldn't keep it together. Her surgeon left very quickly to prepare. I'm not sure what else happened, but I only had minutes. I went to the side of my mom's bed and grabbed her hand. She looked up at me, and I could see in her eyes that she knew it, too. This was it.

Through her tears she started telling me how proud she was of me and that she loved me more than anything. I couldn't handle it. In my mind all I could think was, *No, stop! This is not happening. I will not have this be my goodbye.*

In that second, my whole mindset changed. She would pull through. She would make it. I needed her here. She would get through this. I knew she would. She was strong.

I looked at her and said, "Promise me you'll pull through, Mom." She closed her eyes and started crying even harder. I touched her cheek, and she opened her eyes again. "Mom, promise me."

At that moment the nurses started pushing her bed out of the room to take her into surgery. The last thing my mom whispered to me was, "I promise." I kissed her hand one last time and then, in what seemed like one second, she was already halfway down the hall.

That one promise from her was the only thing that kept me going.

The next four hours or so were a blur. I remember my mom's nurses saying they would keep checking in on me and letting me know how things in surgery were going, but they said the surgery would be around eight hours long. My uncle talked to me for a minute and told me I should go home and rest for a few hours. He said that there was nothing I could do here at the hospital. He would take care of telling the family.

I walked to my car and sat in the parking lot for forty-five minutes. Crying. Crumbling. Processing. Calling my mom's close friend Rebecca was what got me home. She calmed me down. Told me to take deep breaths. I don't remember much after that, but Rebecca said she talked to me from when I started the car until I pulled into my driveway. My brother said I walked inside and went straight to cleaning everything. After about an hour, he said he finally got me to lie down in my bed.

I woke up feeling completely disoriented. How long had I been asleep? What happened? Was last night real? I walked into my mom's room and she was nowhere to be seen. The house was dead silent. On my mom's nightstand I saw her water bottle. The same stupid water bottle she never left the house without. And that's when it hit me.

I crumbled. Fell to my knees and cried harder than I ever had in my life. My grandma found me on my bed about thirty minutes later and said we should probably head to the hospital. I looked at the clock. Nine a.m. How could it only be nine o'clock? My mom had only been in surgery for three hours. It had seemed like eternity.

Trying to make myself look presentable was out of the question, so I threw on some fresh clothes and took off to what was about to be the longest, hardest day of my life.

I had too many missed calls and texts. I tried my best to keep everyone updated. We had so many loved ones praying for her, and the amount of concern was overwhelming. I got to the hospital with family members already waiting there. Friends came and went, giving their love.

Her nurses and surgeons updated us from time to time. Tears. Fear. Anger. Why was this happening to my mom? Why? It wasn't fair. I needed my mom. This wasn't fair at all. I didn't want this life without her in it. I was angry. I was overwhelmed. And most of all, I was distraught.

After hour and hours of waiting with little information, her surgeon came out and took us into a room to talk to us. Family only. I couldn't process anything he was saying. She was alive, but she wasn't out of the woods yet. She was lucky to be alive. They lost her during surgery. Her heart shut down and they had to graft the arteries from her leg onto her heart to get it working again. And the worst, if she wasn't responsive in four to six hours, my mom was brain dead. There was so much more that he said, but I couldn't process any of it. All I knew was I had four hours. I asked him to see her. I needed to do it right away. He told me I could go back to her room in ICU in one hour.

When I walked back and they took me into her room, my heart stopped. I couldn't believe my eyes. My mom was swollen. Every part of her. Her face, her hands, everything. She had a million IVs and tubes coming out of her, and a breathing tube in her mouth. And then there was this huge, clear, blown-up heating pad over her body. What was that for? Her nurse told me they froze her body during the surgery and were bringing it back to a normal temperature.

She looked so scary. Nothing about her resembled the woman I had taken into the ER earlier. *Be strong, McCall. For your brothers. Hold it together.*

We walked out of the ICU, and family and friends flooded us with questions. "How is she? Is she responsive? Give us updates!"

How was I supposed to comfort all of these people when I couldn't even believe it myself? I turned and went straight to the elevator. Any floor. I didn't care, as long as it got me out of there. The third floor bathroom was where I ended up. And for thirty minutes I sat in there. Prayed. Cried. Begged. I was helpless.

When I made it back to the ICU, they said I could go in and see my mom one more time tonight. Did I want to? The heating mat was off. I decided I'd just go look from a distance.

I walked back with her nurse, who smiled at me and said, "I have something I want to show you." I stood at the end of my mom's bed while her nurse went close by her ear and loudly said, "Teri!"

In that instant, my mom's eyes flew open, looked right at me, and closed again.

Tears of joy instantly started flowing. I wanted to kick and scream. She wasn't brain dead! She was responsive! The only good thing that had happened all day. Her nurses said she would need rest and that they would call me to update me on my mom's status, but it was best for us to go home and get some rest.

The next few days were a roller coaster of emotion and heartache. My mom would be doing better one minute, and the next she would be back in surgery. It felt like I lived in that waiting room. More bad news, more bad news, and eventually the good news started coming. My mom was making progress. She was going to live. She was a miracle.

It was months and months of struggle, frustration, and pain. But she did it. My mom lived. She fought. And she recovered. I will never know how truly hard that was on her, but I have never been more grateful to still have my best friend with me here today. I love you, Mom. Thank you for fighting.

ABOUT THE AUTHOR

Teri Benson was born and raised in Logan, Utah. The middle child between two brothers, she grew up spending as much time outdoors as possible. Summer was for water skiing, swimming, and riding motorcycles in the foothills and mountains with her older brother, while winter was for skiing and more skiing. She moved to the Salt Lake area about thirty years ago. She has three amazing kids: Dallin, Jace, and McCall, who are the center of her life.